Decision Equity

Decision Equity

The Ultimate Metric to Connect Marketing Actions to Profits

Piyush Kumar, PhD

Kunal Gupta, PhD

business**expert**
Press

Decision Equity: The Ultimate Metric to Connect Marketing Actions to Profits
Copyright © Business Expert Press, LLC, 2011.

First published in 2011 by
Business Expert Press, LLC
222 East 46th Street, New York, NY 10017
www.businessexpertpress.com

ISBN-13: 978-1-60649-193-5 (paperback)

ISBN-13: 978-1-60649-194-2 (e-book)

DOI 10.4128/9781606491942

A publication in the Business Expert Press Marketing Strategy collection

Collection ISSN: 2150-9654 (print)
Collection ISSN: 2150-9662 (electronic)

Cover design by Jonathan Pennell
Interior design by Scribe Inc.

First edition: March 2011

10 9 8 7 6 5 4 3 2 1

Printed in the United States of America.

Abstract

More than even before, marketers need to justify their decisions by linking them to the corporate bottom line. While this is a challenging task, what makes it more daunting is the absence of a systematic approach and an overarching metric to help make financially sound marketing decisions.

In this new book, Kumar and Gupta resolve both problems. They introduce breakthrough thinking around the financial consequences of marketing actions and propose *decision equity* as the ultimate metric to connect marketing strategies to financial success. Using numerous case studies from small firms to global conglomerates, they provide a comprehensive and robust framework for implementing a *decision equity*–based strategic approach within an organization.

The authors build a compelling case for fact-based decision making and illustrate the power of cross-functional participation in strategic problem solving. They provide a step-by-step approach to build *decision equity*–based systems within firms. They show how organizations can win and achieve their strategic vision by developing a *linkage orientation* and learning how to connect their *Actions to Profits*.

Keywords

Action profit linkage, linkage analysis, decision equity, linkage orientation, customer satisfaction, service quality, return on marketing, customer equity, brand equity

Piyush would like to thank his wife, Shalini, and his daughter, Shivina, for their love and support during the preparation of the manuscript.

Kunal would like to let his wife Rashmi, and his kids, Suhani and Siddhant, know that without their support and patience, this book would not have seen the light of day. He would also like to thank his colleagues and clients that have given him the opportunity to implement his ideas into practice.

Contents

Prologue

The excitement around the boardroom was palpable as department heads streamed in with a shared sense of both victory and optimism. There were plenty of smiles to go around, and warm handshakes and hot coffee were the order of the day. As they slowly settled into their chairs, they chatted about how the firm's stock price had responded favorably to the change in strategy over the last three quarters.

The fortunes of the firm had indeed made an impressive turnaround since the previous vice president of marketing had left. Rumors were that he was judiciously let go because the firm's flagship brand in the marketplace had been steadily slipping and losing share to private labels. The vice president of human resources had launched an aggressive search for a replacement and, in a significant departure from past practice, had strived to and been successful at bringing in someone from outside the industry.

What subsequently transpired reflected a different approach to how the firm did business. The market research process was formalized and the results of extensive customer feedback resulted in a major design change in the packaging of the firm's key product, including a change in the color of the package from yellow to blue. Postlaunch tracking had indicated that customer response to the change was both positive and immediate and had improved the sales per customer by about 50%. The brand was stronger and the private label challenge seemed to have waned.

Today's meeting was to celebrate the firm's recent success and to share thoughts about future strategic moves. The chief executive officer (CEO) walked in with a wide smile on his face and the now familiar and well-known management consultant and advisor at his side. As they settled in and exchanged pleasantries, the CEO gave a general overview of the turnaround at the firm and highlighted the fact that the value of the firm had increased by about $20 million since the time the key strategic change was made to the firm's flagship brand. He then invited each of the departmental heads to give their own perspectives on what had transpired and what the next few steps should be.

The new vice president (VP) of marketing was first and gave an articulate presentation of the major change in the fortunes of the flagship brand. She touted the success of the research-driven approach that had pointed to the brand's key deficiency in packaging and the subsequent strengthening of the brand brought about primarily by the change in the color of the brand's package. She then went on to present the financial consequences of the change in strategy by outlining the dramatic increase in the flagship brand's equity. She explained that she computed the future incremental cash flow that the brand would have generated over a comparable no-name product under the previous strategy. She had calculated the present value of these incremental cash flows using the firm's cost of capital for discounting and called it the baseline *brand equity*. Next, she presented results from a similar analysis using the revised projections of future cash flows under the new brand strategy and called the metric the updated *brand equity*. And there was a mild applause from the CEO when she showed that the change in strategy had increased the equity of the firm's flagship brand by an estimated $20 million, which was very close to the increase in the firm's value over the same period. The VP of marketing enjoyed the moment and took a few questions and suggestions on the future course of the strategy.

The VP of sales stepped up next and shared the details of how the customer response to changes in the firm's strategy had been positive and the sales per customer had registered a significant increase. He then went on to show that the value of an average customer was now much greater than what it had previously been. Interestingly, he said that he had computed the future cash flow per customer under the previous strategy, discounted it, and called it the lifetime value of the customer. He then proceeded to explain how he had aggregated the lifetime value of all the customers and had computed a metric called *customer equity*. Much like the VP of marketing had done, he too had computed the change in the value of *customer equity* following the change in strategy and placed the difference at about $20 million. He hurried through the next slide that showed that the change in the value of the firm could be traced almost entirely to changes in the firm's *customer equity*. The CEO gave him a somewhat confused look and whispered a question into his consultant's ear. The consultant gave a thoughtful glance at the VP of sales but kept quiet.

What followed next was somewhat dramatic. The VP of human resources touted the shift in the firm's hiring strategy and the recruiting of people from outside the industry. She hailed the almost newly minted VP of marketing as a prime example of how the shift had increased the value of the firm by enhancing its *people equity*. By now, the story was clear and the method to compute *people equity* was no different from what those who preceded her had followed. Less surprising was the conclusion that the shift in strategy had enhanced *people equity* by about $20 million, roughly the same amount that firm's value had increased over the same period.

The smile had vanished from the CEO's face, and he was increasingly turning to his consultant to seek clarification regarding what was causing the increase in the value of the firm. Why was it that *brand equity, customer equity*, and *people equity* had gone up to the tune of about $20 million each, yet the firm value was up by only around $20 million? He sent a questioning glance at the chief financial officer (CFO) of the firm and tried to read whether he felt that the truth was better than they thought or that there was less credit to go around than was being claimed. The head of packaging and the chief of market research were yet to make their presentations, and the CEO was trying to guess whether they too would claim returns on packaging and returns on market research to the tune of $20 million each. Was he about to learn about things such as *research equity* and *packaging equity*? As he was lost in his thoughts trying to make sense of all that he had heard, the consultant got up to speak.

PART I
Competing by Verification

CHAPTER 1

Harnessing the Power of Data

Let us begin with a few actual stories to set the tone for the book. The first one is about a leading consumer brand whose managers were perpetually enamored by technological improvements they were making to the products in their portfolio. Not surprisingly, top management had also committed to substantial funds for improving the technology across the product line, a strategy that was well in line with the firm's long-term vision established a few years earlier. Along the way, however, the marketplace underwent dramatic changes. The most significant of these was that the product category in which the company competed was itself increasingly replaced by a better, faster, and cheaper alternative. Despite the writing on the wall, this firm continued to invest millions of dollars in enhancing its existing product portfolio and made no effort to invest in the new technology that was attracting an increasing number of customers. As a result, while the ongoing investments in technology did produce a substantially "improved" product, ironically the product class itself became "irrelevant."

Over time, the market share and financial performance of the firm deteriorated significantly, and its misfortunes continue even to this date. While management did see the train wreck coming its way, nobody stepped up to challenge product policy decisions that were made earlier. There was widespread organizational belief in the strength of the firm's existing product portfolio as well as its customer base. The belief created a flawed assumption among managers that the *technology-driven* product strategy that had served them in the past would continue to work equally well in the future. The marketing problem was exacerbated by the fact that senior management was constrained to planning from quarter to quarter, and long-term investments in an emerging product category seemed too stretched out to be explained to the investor community. Now this is not an isolated example, and we have come across several similar instances including video rental companies investing in redesigning their stores just as customers were migrating to ordering movies from the comfort of their living rooms. Similarly, there are examples of others who invested in superior quality on music CDs even as the market was moving toward downloading music directly from online sources.

Our second story is a very different scenario, which again, in our experience, is quite representative of a wide range of industries. In this case, the firm received thousands of inbound calls from its customers every month across its support centers spread throughout the state it operated in. Following industry practice, each incoming call was routed to the next available support representative, who was trained to make certain inquiries and then take appropriate actions. The call routing system, however, was antiquated and incapable of differentiating among calls from high-value versus low-value customers. To make matters worse, the representatives were not given any training or advice on how to handle the two groups of customers differentially. Instead, the focus was on *cost containment* and productivity—which led to the representatives attempting to maximize the number of calls handled per hour. They were also instructed to be strict about reneging late payment and other similar fines—a big reason for customer calls in the first place.

Senior management treated these call centers strictly as cost centers. It was insistent on keeping costs down through higher employee productivity and minimal cancellation of penalties and fees. Therefore, when a call came into the call center, the representatives treated the high- as well as the low-value customer groups in an identical fashion for all issues ranging from late payment to bill correction. A customer who had paid sizeable bills on time for the last several years but missed one payment because of a vacation was treated identically to another with a recurring record of missed or late payments. Not surprisingly, the system resulted in an exodus of a large number of the high-value customers who were always being solicited by competitors. Over time, the firm was left with a substantially less profitable customer base.

These remaining customers had a shorter tenure and smaller lifetime value, and the firm faced greater uncertainty in the cash flows expected from this pool. To make matters worse, given the high level of service required by these customers, the firm continues to spend a lot on servicing their needs. Suggestions to update the call center infrastructure to link a customer's value and payment history to the incoming call identification or the account number of the customer have been ignored for years. Now in an environment of belt tightening, these investments, or "costs" as senior managers often call them, are even more difficult to justify to investors, and the status quo is maintained. Management continues to treat the call centers as mere cost centers and gauges their performance solely on metrics of productivity and cost containment. New investments in these locations contradict management belief, while the firm continues to see an exodus of its high-value customers. From an external observer's perspective, even a cursory look at the data makes it painfully obvious that customer exodus often follows an unsatisfactory call center interaction, but the faith and belief in a well-established, productivity-driven model continues to drive decisions even in the face of compelling evidence to the contrary.

Finally, in a somewhat similar but generalized example, we often find that retail firms emphasize *productivity* in their individual stores. These productivity improvements are believed to have a strong positive impact on the financial performance of the firm. However, a recent engagement with one such retail firm suggests that caution should be exercised when boarding the "productivity wagon." Productivity improvements, especially beyond a critical point, often lead to compromises in the level of service quality experienced by customers. For example, customers experience great resentment when they find fewer employees available to help them in these so-called productive stores and fewer stock-keeping units to choose from within a "rationalized" product assortment. While such adverse customer experiences are often not obvious in the short term, they lead to an erosion of customer loyalty in the long term. Extensive work, done by the American Customer Satisfaction Index (ACSI)[1] research team, also supports our observation, where they find that service companies, such as airlines, often score below manufacturing organizations in the ACSI report card. This poor performance can often be attributed to attempts made by these firms to boost their productivity levels. Interestingly, these strategic choices are often not made in isolation but are the result of boarding the *benchmarking* bandwagon. Management feels the pressure to match its industry peers on select metrics, including those related to productivity, without giving deep thought to the ultimate consequences of adopting common industry practices and metrics. The underlying assumption, which we find often seriously flawed, is that not everyone within the industry can be wrong, especially when the short-term financial merit of emulating them can be observed relatively quickly. For example, we often read statistics about the "instantaneous" extra revenue airlines make because of new baggage fees, food for sale on board, and the removal of pillows and blankets from their aircrafts. However, we seldom hear about the potential adverse long-term consequences of such choices.

Our interactions with thousands of managers, consultants, management students, and academic thought leaders suggest that such stories can go on endlessly. In fact, we find that every day, a large number of managers make decisions based on intuition, entrenched mental beliefs, or knee-jerk reactions to competitive actions, without pausing to seek empirical support or validation. While observing the inner workings of big and small businesses, we have been a regular witness to the execution of beliefs-based decisions that rely on untested and unvalidated assumptions. Even as we write this book, we can find many senior leaders who continue to place extreme levels of confidence in the benefits of their unwavering beliefs in a variety of performance drivers, including *innovation, cost control, productivity, benchmarking*, and many more. In addition, the long-term effects of decisions that generate a positive short-term return, such as higher customer fees and lower levels of customer service, are seldom tested or validated.

The corporate world seems to have little time to pause and think and plan for fact-based decision making, for fear that nervous investors are ever so willing to abandon the ship and invest in alternatives. Such short and finite periods also correspond with the finite tenure of top management within most organizations. For example, in 2005, about 6 in 10 chief executive officers (CEOs) of Standard and Poor's (S&P) 500 firms had less than 6 years in their jobs as CEO.[2] In addition, as is well known, these leaders are evaluated and remunerated based on financial results produced *during* their tenure. This short-term orientation exacerbates the problem and the vision, and decision making at the top remains myopic. In such an environment, rapid fire, beliefs-based decision making continues to thrive at the expense of fact-based and data-driven decisions that possibly require longer periods of incubation and an alternative strategic mind-set.

The Data Deluge

Yes, we could give these decision makers some benefit of the doubt. We could possible argue that, even if they wanted to, these managers might not have ready access to data to test and verify their hypotheses. Alternately, we could reason that the data are actually available to test management beliefs and their mental models but are not deployed effectively while making key strategic and tactical decisions. While until a few years ago, it might have been possible to make a case for the absence of good quality data, a number of recently published studies suggest that high-quality data are now widely available. Most organizations today live in an extremely data-rich environment. Recently reported statistics[3] suggest that over 160 exabytes (1 exabyte = 10^{18} bytes) of digital data were generated worldwide in 2006. This is the equivalent to 36 billion digital movies, 43 trillion digital songs, or 1 million digital copies of *every* book in the Library of Congress. In 2006, these books would represent about 6 tons of books for every man, woman, and child on earth—approximately the weight of a large adult elephant. By the end of 2010, this number was expected to grow to about 1,000 exabytes at a whopping 57% compounded annual growth rate and was projected to outpace the capacity to store such data. Another way to think of this volume of data is that in 2006, the digital universe was the equivalent of 12 stacks of books extending from the earth to the sun, or one stack of books twice around the earth's orbit. By the end of 2010, the stack of books could reach from the Sun to Pluto and back![4]

While a lot of the information, such as digital entertainment, is for consumer consumption, it is also generated by various for-profit and non-profit organizations through customer relationship management (CRM) systems, internal metrics and processes, as well as external organizational measures of sales and competitive activities. In 2006, about 25% of the worldwide digital data were generated in the workplace—approximately 40 exabytes. By the end of 2010, this volume is expected to rise to about 30%—about 300 exabytes. Wal-Mart's gargantuan database, for instance, has grown from 110 terabytes in 2000 (1 terabyte = 10^{12} bytes) to half a petabyte in 2004 (1 petabyte = 10^{21} bytes). These data are generated primarily to support internal decisions and provide information to other partners, such as suppliers in the value chain. The point is that an absence of adequate and readily available data no longer seems to be a justifiable reason for the pattern of intuition-based decision making that is rampant among various layers of management today. Instead, it is perhaps time for them to leverage the vast amounts of well-structured data at their disposal and to hone their skills to make more effective decisions.

Critical Leadership Skill

We believe that in this environment of data sufficiency and perhaps excess, coupled with the impatience of the investor community, a key managerial skill is the ability to sift through piles of data and hone in on those pieces of information that are most critical to organizational success. This requires decision makers to be quick and articulate in summarizing the situations they face, to convert them into sets of formal or informal hypotheses, to identify the data requirements to test the hypotheses, and then to make strategic calls at high speed.

For example, let us say that you are the country manager for a quick-serve restaurant in an emerging market. At the current juncture in the organizational evolution, you are faced with the task of increasing your market penetration. One morning, you hear unexpected and potentially game-changing news that a key competitor has big plans of entering the marketplace! Being from the trade, you recognize the competitor's likely entry strategy, but at best, it is an intelligent guess. What would you do? Would you make changes to your prices to attract more customers? How would you assess if you could afford it? Alternatively, would you seek greater retail outlet penetration? How would you know if you can find good sites at a fast pace? Would you spend more on advertising? Would you make changes to your menu items? Or would you do some combination of these possible reactions, or do nothing? Can all the learning from brand equity, segmentation, category and brand awareness, and pricing studies aid you? Think fast—time is running out!

How can this be done? While we will go into the details of the answer to this question, we will briefly illustrate the importance of this critical skill using a simple example. In this case, a large and financially distressed firm appointed a new president. He was an outsider to the industry, but had a proven record of successfully turning around companies. Most of the employees in the firm looked forward to his arrival and the excitement was palpable. Recent market research had indicated that the firm was losing customers at a much faster pace than usual and that its brand was losing its equity. In order to quickly hone in on the problem, the new appointee immediately offered to spend a few days with the consumer insights group to identify key areas of focus that could help the firm deliver superior customer experiences and rebuild the brand. After all, the insights group had spent considerable time and money on various studies and was most likely to have an answer. The group presented multiple studies to him and he listened to each one of them patiently. At the conclusion of each presentation, there were recommendations on potential areas of investment toward building a stronger marketplace presence for the brand.

When the presentations ended, he congratulated the group for sharing the work and posed one simple question: While each presenter had provided good ideas, if all of them were intended to create more satisfied customers and a stronger brand, why was it that the recommendations had no synergy? Each study asked for investing in a completely different area of performance, and he was now even more confused than when he started. He had a pool of funds budgeted for strengthening the brand and the customer experience but was not sure of the best way to deploy them.

In this case, the leader demonstrated two of the critical leadership skills we are referring to. The first was a faith in information and data to solve strategic problems. The second was recognition of the limitations of a set of unrelated, albeit data-driven, solutions without a unifying synergistic framework. To help resolve the problem, the firm worked toward integrating the numerous pieces of existing feedback from the marketplace and building a unifying framework around them. The estimated impact of each proposed initiative was then linked to monetary value. It created a common metric to compare different investment alternatives. With the help of the overall framework to synthesize the information from the various studies, and the estimated bottom-line impact of each, the new president was able to compare alternate initiatives using common evaluative criteria. He could prioritize them and draw linkages among them. For example, he could see how clearer communication during the presale and the sales processes could minimize customer confusion and reduce the volume of expensive inbound calls. He could draw similar linkages between the quality of the billing process and the rate of customer defection. And most important, he could append estimates of returns on investment for each potential area of improvement. As a result, he was ultimately in a position to make informed, coherent, and data-driven decisions after accounting for their firm-wide strategic and financial impact.

Rising Cost of Errors

In these opening remarks, we would also like to allude to the viral impact of failed decisions in today's information-rich and interconnected environment. Corporate errors are instantly visible in a world of global communication and are increasingly less pardonable. Consumers, advocates, activists, and citizens at large get information at their fingertips almost instantly, which in turn can have serious repercussions for organizational survival. For example, a quick Google search for "Toyota brake problems" generated about 4 million links on the web, while the search for "BP oil spill" generated 387 million links.[5] Before the Deepwater Horizon rig exploded and sank on April 20, 2010, BP was Britain's biggest company with a stock market value of 122 billion pound sterling, and by June 10, 2010, the oil spill wiped out 47%, or roughly 50 billion pound sterling, of its value. And this may not completely reflect the erosion of customer goodwill, loss of human lives, cleanup effort costs, and countless payments and retributions that may follow. While the exact cause of the spill is still unknown, someone somewhere perhaps made a decision that eroded half the value of the company in a matter of days.

While the consequences of the BP oil disaster are somewhat immediate, the erosion of a firm's equity in the marketplace, in many cases, could be slow and silent. Consumers vent on the web and on social media sites, and the epidemic can travel rapidly to other current and potential consumers. According to a study published by Forrester Research and Intelliseek in 2006, recommendations from other consumers, through consumer-generated media, were the most trusted form of advertising vis-à-vis other popular sources of advertising. More than 4 in 5 respondents claimed trusting the recommendations that other consumers made on various products and services. And then there are numerous case studies of consumers venting their frustration on the web, which went viral in a matter of hours. All it takes for such information to be created and widespread is an unpleasant moment of truth, or one wrong decision made by an individual employee. In reality though, some of it is unavoidable—a chain is only as strong as the weakest link. And that weakest link could be a bad decision made with good intent—an employee who thought he was being helpful to the customer but was perceived otherwise or somebody somewhere refusing to accede to a seemingly unjustified customer demand that then blew out of proportion.

The purpose of the subsequent chapters in this book is not to propose a method to avoid all such errors. An error-free organizational performance is perhaps not a realistic or attainable goal. Further, sometimes the criticality of a quick decision leads to an expedited decision-making process where little time might be available to gather and process the necessary information. However, where possible, managers and front-line workers should tap into vast amounts of data that are available to them to provide justification and validation for their decisions. Decisions based on beliefs and without forethought rather than empirical validation would continue to adversely affect organizations and erode their value. We propose that decision makers can do much better than this!

CHAPTER 2

The Cost of Intuition-Based Decision Making

The analogy is not new, but running a large organization is indeed like flying a complex airplane requiring a sophisticated operating and control system for navigation. The top leadership team at the head of the organization has a targeted destination in mind and is responsible for both charting the most appropriate course and navigating the organization along it. This destination may be broadly defined in terms of a long-term return on assets or in more specific terms, such as a desired strategic position in a product market or a successful outcome of a vital new product development project.

Along the way, the team uses a set of markers or indicators that signal whether the organization is on course to reaching its final destination or is veering off course. The purpose of these indicators is to assess whether the progress being made toward the destination is adequate or if any corrective action is warranted to navigate around unforeseen circumstances or undesirable outcomes. Therefore, the markers are selected in a way that keeping a watch of them is analogous to keeping an eye on the business and ensuring that it is progressing toward the intended goal.

Now imagine what would happen if the crew of an aircraft knew its final destination but did not know the exact course to chart. Imagine what would happen if it knew the functions of the various levers and indicators in the cockpit but not how they related to each other or to reaching the final target. Under such circumstances, the crew might sometimes make it to its destination or land in the vicinity and at other times might miss it completely. It might sometimes try out a few maneuvers to see which one works and might be able to fly the plane generally in the intended direction through trial and error. And even if it was somehow able to bring a wavering aircraft under control, it may not learn which lever or a combination of levers ultimately did the trick. Conversely, if the aircraft was veering off course, the crew might not know exactly how to navigate it back in the intended direction. Ultimately, whether the final outcome is favorable or adverse, the crew might discover little regarding exactly which combination of actions works and which ones to take if the circumstances repeated themselves or if a new set of challenging circumstances presented themselves.

While this might sound scary, many organizations today find themselves in a similar situation. Their executive leadership tends to have an approximate idea of where it wants to take the organization but often does not have a clear path laid out for getting there. Their senior management teams generally understand the strategic and tactical levers that are at their disposal but do not necessarily have a coherent idea regarding how these levers independently or jointly relate to the ultimate outcome, such as short- or long-term profitability.

This lack of a full understanding of the relationship between the choices made and the resulting outcomes tends to tie organizations to a fate that is suboptimal at best and catastrophic at worst. For example, an organization with one of the most recognizable brands in the world was experiencing some serious erosion in its brand equity in the marketplace. Senior management therefore made a push to restore the customers' awareness of and confidence in the brand. However, this important initiative stayed completely independent of a review of customer loyalty in the marketplace. The organization had a silo structure where two independent teams managed the brand equity and the customer loyalty programs respectively. With virtually *no* communication between the two teams, it became impossible for the organization to recognize that bolstering its brand would be a tall order when its customers were fleeing to competition. The chief marketing officer (CMO) did not recognize the *relationship* between the brand and customer loyalty and did not want the customer loyalty team to touch his "important" brand initiative. The organization's silo-based structure fostered an environment where it became impossible for top management to accept customer loyalty as potentially a key pillar of a strong brand. Unfortunately, the brand continues to see depletion in its equity even as of today.

Another way to think of such situations is to imagine a complex electric circuit where one has access to an array of switches that are somehow linked to a sequence of small bulbs and finally to a bright large bulb. Imagine that some combinations of switches light up one or more of the small bulbs and indicate how close one is to lighting the large one. But only a few combinations of switches actually light it up. Suppose that one does not have the ability to map which set of switches relate to each of the small bulbs or how the set of small bulbs relate to the final bright one. In other words, imagine what would happen if one does not have the ability to trace the pathways from the switches at one end to the bright bulb at the other. This is exactly the problem many organizations face today.

In the absence of precise information regarding the structure of relationships between the levers under their control and their ultimate corporate goals, managers tend to overly rely on their gut feelings or a set of assumptions regarding causation. They *believe* that certain specific paths are most likely to lead to desirable outcomes. And by way of consistency, they also believe in certain selected markers being true indicators of progress being made toward the goal along the pathway of choice. For example, we find that managers are often committed to specific pathways such as those characterized by innovation, superior product design, deeper customer relationships, leveraged capital structure, or employee retention without truly understanding whether these are indeed the best ways to reach their ultimate financial goals. And in order to be consistent with their beliefs, these managers choose markers, such as relative design superiority, customer loyalty, capital structure, or employee engagement as the appropriate measures of their success along the chosen path. This reliance on strong prior beliefs and an absence of verification tends to suppress the search for alternative strategic pathways and often results in suboptimal or even undesirable business strategies.

Managerial Decision Making

Every day, managers face problems that lack a clear solution or even a clear path to finding one. How they individually articulate these problems and search for solutions has a profound impact on whether or not they are able to achieve their desired goals either completely or even partially. So just put yourself in the shoes of these managers and think back to the last time you faced an important organizational decision. Now ask yourself which of the following scenarios best exemplifies the situation you found yourself in:

1. You had *all* the information needed to make the decision, including clarity of objectives, which allowed you to evaluate all possible alternatives objectively and reach an unbiased and fact-based decision.
2. You had *some* information available and some missing, but you trusted your intuition and experience and settled on the first alternative that seemed satisfactory or reasonable.
3. Conflicting objectives of various stakeholders influenced your decision making, and few facts were available to support the chosen alternative.
4. The decision-making process seemed haphazard and unpredictable, and the chosen alternative was an outcome of trial and error.

There is better than an even chance that you would claim that your decision-making process was fairly close to the first alternative. You may be swayed into grudgingly acknowledging that it also had some elements of the second alternative. You would perhaps also agree that all stakeholders impacted by the decision were made to believe in the rigor that went into the decision-making process and that external constituents, such as consultants, vetted the foundations of the methodology used to arrive at the decision. Deep inside your own conscience though, you will perhaps have a nagging suspicion that the third and the fourth options are closer to the truth, and you might recall hoping that somehow the facts you considered and presented then came together as a coherent, fact-based story.

This is not surprising at all. Every day, millions of presentations are made in the corporate world, each of which attempts to present the answer to a problem or share an opportunity. Most resemble one of the four decision-making scenarios described at the beginning of this chapter. These decisions can range from frequent operational choices to the relatively infrequent strategic choices that have a critical impact on the health and survival of an organization. Common examples of operational decisions include deciding if late fees should be waived for customers, selecting the number of employees to staff in the restaurant in anticipation of a high-traffic weekend, or ordering the appropriate quantity of raw materials in anticipation of future demand. Examples of strategic decisions, on the other hand, include long-term price formatting decisions, entry into new markets, and service workforce reduction during lean economic times.

The fact that the process of making an organizational decision has an impact on the likely success of the resulting outcome is well documented. Past evidence shows that as high as 50% of managerial decisions made in organizations either fail or are suboptimal.[1] In other words, the performance of an average manager is at best about as good as a flip of a coin—they are right one half of the time and partly or completely wrong the other half of the time. While the errors from some of these decisions are visible within a short span of time, others come to haunt organizations many years later. A lot can therefore change between the time a strategic choice is made and its ultimate outcome is realized. For example, the real impact of a loosening of the lending policy that qualifies less than creditworthy homeowners for mortgages may be seen years after the policy is first instituted.

The excuse that external constraints negatively influence the outcomes of even good decisions has limited face validity. There is evidence that suggests that, even in the presence of constraints, managers retain a substantial degree of control over their decisions. One very obvious support for this position comes from the observation that while some managers make poor choices leading to devastating consequences for the firm during extenuating external circumstances, others make much better choices and attain superior relative performance. Such variation could not exist if the external constraints alone were driving these choices. So pointing to the external circumstances and external adversities as the drivers of suboptimal decisions has little evidence to back it up.

Alternate Models of Decision Making

The four decision-making processes listed above, while not mutually exclusive, point to alternate models of decision making observed in organizations. We briefly discuss the merits and limitations of each of these here. In its most basic form, the "rational model of decision making" suggests that decision makers solve problems with very clearly defined objectives. These objectives are typically specified in terms of the direction and magnitude of change in one or more organizational metrics. For example, the objective tied to a decision regarding whether or not to invest in sales force training may be driven by an overall metric such as a reduction in customer churn. The selection of the metric might itself be driven by an assumed set of directional relationships such as the following:

sales training → improved sales force knowledge of products → higher sales force engagement → better customer experience → improvement in customer loyalty → reduction in customer churn

Equipped with such objectives, the decision makers then gather appropriate information and develop a set of alternate options. They eventually select an appropriate action option based on a logical and systematic comparison of the alternatives. This model of decision making, informed by classic economic theory, is rooted in the assumption that decision makers are completely rational in their approach. Of course, some of these assumptions, like those that follow, make the model somewhat unrealistic because they ignore the reality of time constraints, limits to human knowledge, and finite information-processing capabilities:

- The decision maker is aware of *all* alternatives.
- The decision maker can *compute* the odds of success for each alternative under consideration.
- The decision maker uses a very *rational*, evidence-based process to choose the best alternative.
- Political or other organizational considerations do not influence the outcome.

Now while every organization would like to follow the "rational model of decision making," it cannot, because the approach requires limitless availability of resources, such as time, as well as complete knowledge of all available alternatives. It also assumes limitless capacity of the decision maker to gather and process information. Therefore, it is very unlikely that the rational model would be an applied model of decision making within most organizations. Think of a seemingly simple problem of menu optimization in a quick-serve restaurant (QSR) environment. A typical QSR menu can consist of over 60 items with many constraints existing between the prices of items on a menu as well as the presence or absence of individual menu items. For example, it would be very unlikely that the restaurant would offer a sandwich in a combo meal that it would not offer on the menu as a single sandwich. Also, the combo meal would have to be priced so that it is less than or equal to the sum of the individual menu items that compose the meal. In addition, QSRs have various size offerings for side items and drinks, requiring consumers to pay more for larger sized items but often not in proportion to the increase in size. Looking to optimize both the share of visits and the average ticket spent per visit by configuring which products should appear on the menu at what price requires running hundreds of millions of various menu configurations, all of which adhere to the traditional pricing and availability norms for a QSR menu. Computing the results for a single menu takes upward of 15 minutes, so time becomes an issue for running all possible menu configurations. The "rational model of decision making" is therefore best regarded as a theoretical limit, rather than a feasible and implementable option.

On the other end of the spectrum, the decision-making process in organizations can be viewed as extremely haphazard and unpredictable, where decisions appear completely random and unsystematic. The "garbage can model of decision making" views the organization in a chaotic state where problems, solutions, participants, and available opportunities float around randomly. If the four factors happen to connect, a decision is made. This model describes decision making as operating in highly ambiguous settings or "organized anarchies"—organizations that are beset by extreme ambiguity that surfaces in three principal ways described subsequently. The key assumptions under such a decision-making process are the following:

- Presence of inconsistent and ill-defined preferences of the decision makers
- Lack of a clear understanding of cause and effect and gain in organizational knowledge by participants' trial and error
- Fluid entry and exit of decision-making participants from the decision process, with their involvement depending on their energy, interest, and other demands on their time

The garbage can model calls attention to the importance of chance, wherein what gets decided depends very strongly on timing and luck. While organizations can survive this chance approach during benevolent times, more trying times highlight the shortcoming of such an approach. Moreover, decisions have a fuzzy character—they lack clear start and end points and individuals are unsure of the objectives and change their minds often. One would hope that one's own organization does not have a semblance of the "garbage can model of decision making" and that the decisions have some clarity of objectives, a somewhat systematic process of identifying cause and effects, and that decision makers do better than random trial and error.

The "political behavior" model of decision making is recognized as a little more real and valid reflection of organizational decision making. The two key ideas underlying the political dimension of decision making are the following:

• People in organizations have differences in incentives result-ing from functional, hierarchical, professional, and personal interests.
• People in organizations try to influence the outcomes of deci-sions, so that their own interests are served, and they do so by using a variety of political techniques.

The presence of functional silos in organizations and friction among these silos is seen as a dominant cause of differences in interest among various stakeholders. Friction comes from competition among the silos for the common pool of organizational resources. Local groups of decision mak-ers then engage in a zero-sum game, where the success of one silo is seen as the defeat of another. Rarely do they come together to seek coopera-tion and synergy toward achieving larger organizational goals. As might be obvious, such behavior reduces the effectiveness of strategic decision making, yet is accepted as a reality of corporate culture. From a com-parison perspective, while the "garbage can model" ignores the cognitive capability of decision makers, the "political model" assumes that people are superheroes capable of calculating and implementing comprehensive political strategies to further their personal goals and interests.

Given the limitations of the various decision-making models, as well as a realization that objectives can be inconsistent across people and over time, the "bounded rationality model of decision making" seems to be a more realistic description of organizational decision making. This model, proposed by Herbert Simon, won him the Nobel Prize in 1978. The key premise of this model is that there are constraints that lead a decision maker to be less than completely rational while making decisions. Managers therefore often search for information and alternatives opportunistically. The model therefore realizes that managers *satisfice*—that is, select the first alternative that seems good enough, because the costs of seeking an optimal solution are impractical in terms of the required time and effort. Analysis of alternatives might thus be limited, and decisions may often not use a completely systematic analysis. The following are the four key assumptions of this model:

- Managers make decisions by rules of thumb or heuristics.
- Managers are comfortable making decisions without determining all the alternatives.
- Managers select the first alternative that is satisfactory.
- Managers realize that their conception of the world is satisfactory.

The model therefore assumes that managers develop shortcuts, called *heuristics*, to make decisions that are largely driven by what has worked in the past. Managers might thus develop multiple alternatives, even though cursorily, and then analyze them to some degree, relying on past experience to select the first seemingly acceptable alternative. Over a period of time, heuristics-based decision making can transform into intuition-based decision making, where such "intuition represents a collection of what we have learned about the world, without knowing that we have actually learned it."[2] Managers then develop intuition-based mental models that they bring to bear across repeated problem solving opportunities. Consequently, in many cases, the primary reason for building strategy around the implementation of existing mental models is that they pass a face validity test. They sound and feel right and do not conflict with one's intuition around how things should work.

The Case for Managerial Intuition

In the absence of a formal or an informal system that outlines the relationships among the choices made and the series of interrelated possible outcomes that might result, managers tend to rely on their belief systems or commonly accepted models of how actions relate to effect. As they apply these models repeatedly and are even partially successful, their initial beliefs become self-fulfilling, and managers become even more confident in the applicability of these models. Ultimately, the models entrench themselves in the decision-making process, and managers become risk averse to deviating from the principles they initially believed in and found some evidence for.

Therefore, one can make a case for sticking to a few basic principles that simplify complex problems and lend them some level of tractability. It might often be preferable to get a solution that is approximate and somewhat correct than to invest in trying to find an almost correct solution but never getting close. And of course, if the decision domain is relatively simple, and the consequences of actions can be determined with a high level of accuracy, there is a stronger case that can be made for relying on straight and simple principles and following one's intuition.

To that extent, strategic intuition perhaps does bring certain efficiency to the decision-making process by helping eliminate obviously unviable alternatives or short-listing those that are clearly viable. For example, the management at one retail bank had the strategic intuition to continue to monitor the levels of satisfaction among its top 1% wealthiest customers. In the past, some managers at this firm had raised questions regarding the resources invested into such measurement, and their challenge was perhaps well founded. Despite sincere efforts to work on the recommendations of such research in the past few years, the organization had seen very little improvement in the satisfaction scores of these wealthy customers. This encouraged the skeptics to challenge the continued investment in an effort that was apparently not bearing fruit. The proponents however stood by their strategic intuition that it was critical to understand and work on issues that were important to who they believed was a very important set of customers.

Over time, the data supported the unwavering intuition of the proponents. When we linked customer loyalty data to the financial activity data of these customers, we found that even small increments in satisfaction scores, such as those observed in the past, led to substantial financial windfall for the bank. These were one of the wealthiest sets of customers and therefore cognizant of the level of service they could and should get from their bank. Therefore, even if the bank did everything that it thought it needed to do to please these customers, these individuals, on average, were not elated. However, even if the satisfaction-enhancing initiatives were able to favorably affect a few of these individuals, the amount of incremental business generated for the bank was significant. Had these senior executives ignored their strategic intuition and acceded to the calls for dropping the measurement program, the bank could have seriously jeopardized the amount of business it was able to generate from its high-value customers.

Further, from an organizational perspective, following commonly accepted principles does bring a coherence to the strategy team if its members share the same mental models of what makes the business work or how the strategic choices relate to consequences. In work within support environments, for example, we have found strong agreement among executives for positive and significant linkages between measures of employee engagement, process effectiveness, and customer experience. The data almost always support their beliefs. We do find empirical evidence that higher levels of employee engagement lead to a greater ability of such employees to fix problems the first time and on time. Together, more effective problem resolution coupled with the behaviors associated with more engaged employees, such as greater professionalism and product knowledge, lead to superior customer experiences. Having verified such linkages, these organizations can easily assess the impact of key operational metrics on customer experience. Subsequently, strategic questions, such as evaluating the impact that a 5% improvement in employee engagement levels has on the level of customer experience, become meaningful and relevant. The level of impact can then be compared with other alternative initiatives, such as a 5% improvement in the first-time-fix rate to allow management to take actions that optimize returns on invested resources.

Overall, there is perhaps nothing wrong in making higher order strategic choices based on managerial intuition. In most cases, these intuitive choices evolve from some form of due diligence or historical experience. The due diligence covers marketing, operational, and financial realities using processes that capture the dynamics of the sector or the industry, the unique characteristics of the firm, or the specific decision domain. The historical experience takes advantage of applying previous learning from dealing with similar problems to newer problems.

However, our experience suggests that a majority of managers are hard-pressed to convincingly plot the causal chains from any of these choices to long-term firm profitability. They might be able to provide the logic for these choices and provide supporting evidence that is directionally consistent with it, but in most cases, they are unable to lay out the sequence of events or outcomes that will connect their actions with the ultimate desired outcomes. For example, they often point to evidence that strong brands tend to have greater market share or that social networks provide insights into customers' thinking and help build deeper customer relationships. But they are hard-pressed to link these pieces of intuition to an actual sequence of events, or to tie them to a series of specific metrics that point to superior business performance.

This no longer comes to us as a surprise because the discovery and establishment of connections between the actions taken by an organization and the sequence of outcomes produced by them requires a considerable investment of resources. It also requires a strategic vision on the part of top management and a desire to see how different sets of measures inform each other. It needs mental tenacity because the findings often fly in the face of established organizational beliefs but can provide some very valuable actionable information to the organization. For example, in an engagement with a call center operation, we attempted to establish linkages between two key performance metrics—on-time fix (OTF) and first-time fix (FTF)—and downstream performance. The data provided strong evidence of linkages between the FTF measure and customer perceptions of their transaction. In other words, customers who had their problems fixed the first time were more likely to report favorable evaluations of the call center support transaction. What intrigued us however was the lack of support for a similar relationship between OTF and customer perceptions. We found that customers who had their problems solved "on-time" reported unfavorable evaluations of their support transaction.

The analysis prompted further investigation that revealed the reason for this discrepancy. OTF, as coded in the internal databases of the organization, referred to the organization's ability to resolve the issue as per its own *internal* benchmarks. These benchmarks, established years ago, had never been revised, despite the more recent advent of competitors who were very likely to fix problems much sooner. Customer expectations had therefore evolved, and the organization's internal standards and the reality of the marketplace were no longer aligned. As a result, even though the organization continued to laud its OTF performance, it did nothing to enhance the quality of the customer experience. Since the discovery of the linkages between these metrics and customer impression, the organization has revised its OTF definition and has aligned it with the updated customer expectations.

The True Cost of Intuition

While strategic intuition and mental models are valuable and bring common overarching themes to assist managers in making decisions, there is potentially a strong downside to relying on them across the board. We find that this cost of intuition tends to remain hidden if the business landscape is relatively benevolent. When the times are good, organizations with both good and bad strategies survive and flourish because the external conditions provide a floor to poor performance. However, in the long run, or when times get tough, it is only prudent and considered strategic choices that lead to sustained market and financial performance. So how does one discover these prudent decisions? Does one really need to go beyond the routine due diligence that one follows when making key strategic choices? Is there a need to go beyond the mental models that influence decisions such as market entry, capacity planning, investment commitment, or competence development?

We believe the answer to these questions is a resounding yes. The decision making among the top leadership or the senior managers that constitute strategy teams is often constrained by two sets of factors. The first is the availability of well-processed information that helps them predict the impact of their choice alternatives over a period of time. For example, the top management at a firm might be contemplating a rationalization of its brand portfolio. While it will be able to assess the strength of each brand in the markets it serves and the product lines it supports, it will be hard-pressed to predict, at least over the long run, what the precise consequences of the rationalization process might be. And of course, it might even be difficult to pin down precisely what rationalization really means and what the possible branding scenarios that are either better or worse than the status quo really are.

The second factor is that top management does not have an overarching model that would tie all the available information coherently and parsimoniously and use data to connect actions to outcomes in order to separate good choices from bad ones. For example, a grocery chain might want to enhance productivity in its stores, a very common action undertaken during tough economic times. One option to increase such productivity might come from reducing the number of employees in each of its retail outlets. Such employee reduction can however have two counter forces. From a cost perspective, it can reduce semivariable costs immediately and lead to higher profits. However, from a customer experience perspective, it might lead to inferior customer trips, as more irate customers might need to wait longer at the checkout lines and find it tougher to locate an in-store employee to help them with their needs. This might lead to customer exodus over time, and therefore a reduction in the profits of these stores. The firm therefore needs to understand the nature and size of these two counter forces and identify if the net impact will lead to the desired results.

Management and their strategists compensate for this lack of information or the ability to forge it together by relying on mental models that include heuristics or simple rules of thumb. These mental models come in many shapes and forms and draw upon conventional wisdom in the industry, individual and collective past experiences of the management team, domain-specific data analyses, and good old-fashioned intuition. For example, the management models might create a link between productivity enhancements and a boost in profits based on some short-term observation from the past, and use it as a generalization of their business model. The strategy team might then rely on analogy to make a connection between past implementation of the mental models and their applicability to a current situation.

Consequently, in many cases, the primary reason for building strategy around the implementation of existing mental models is that they pass a face validity test. They sound and feel right and do not conflict with one's intuition about how things should work. For example, a popular mental model is that product design should center on customer preferences because doing so will increase market share and reduce the cost of maintaining the customer base. The model sounds right, is believable, appears universally applicable, and easily passes the face validity test. How would one argue against its central premise? Managers then connect such mental models to a set of levers that need to be pulled in order to drive business performance. Additionally, sometimes a simple set of measures is identified and used to provide rudimentary quantitative support to the underlying mental model.

However, the outcomes from pulling strategic levers are often realized over a long period. For example, the real impact of a loosening of the lending policy that qualifies homeowners for mortgages may be seen years after the policy is instituted. A lot can change between the time a strategic choice is made and the outcome is realized. These changes could be in the external circumstances as well as the way the strategy is implemented within the firm. In the technology sector, for example, the successful choice of investing in a new technology is contingent on the ability to execute the plan quickly, before competition introduces a similar or a better offering. The pace of these changes can and does outpace the speed at which mental models themselves evolve. Consequently, as things change, there is an urge to fit the new realities into the old or existing mental models and somehow manage the business with the same set of levers.

More importantly, an unintended consequence of persistence with or a repeated implementation of a small set of mental models is that they gradually perpetuate both within and across firms and ultimately get embedded in their core belief structures. They form a common fabric of strategic intuition that everyone from individual managers to divisions to the entire firm and even the industry as a whole resort to when faced with a choice in the domain where the model is set. Over time, organizations rely increasingly on the intuition surrounding these models to solve simple to complex problems. The perpetuation and a lack of continuous verification of these mental models can often result in a destructive cycle that ultimately traps organizations into a strategy prison. And unless an organization adopts a concerted approach to break free, it would continue to fit the realities of today with the intuition-based lessons of yesteryears.

CHAPTER 3

Ten Questions to Ask Your Mental Models

Most strategic models are not universally applicable across contexts and over time. We believe that each model has a certain "half-life" and its utility declines gradually over time as it is replaced by a newer generation of models. For example, as technology has evolved and banks have increasingly mechanized customer transactions through automatic teller machines or over the Internet, the definition of what constitutes a customer experience has evolved dramatically. The appropriate strategic model of competing on service quality or on distribution strength has also evolved in parallel. However, not every firm has aligned itself with this evolution at the same pace. While some have pioneered new business models to capitalize on the pace of technology, others have been insensitive to the half-life of the old business model and are trapped in their legacy systems.

These principles of legacy are entrenched at various levels inside organizations. At one end, they are a part of the mental makeup of individuals. For example, we worked with two successive divisional heads within the same large enterprise. The second one headed the division after the first one retired. However, because of somewhat different sets of experiences, they believed in two mutually opposing business models of sales enhancement. The first believed in what marketers traditionally refer to as consumer pull and preferred to invest divisional resources into brand building and customer centricity. In sharp contrast, his successor had immense faith in what is referred to as a push strategy and believed that developing strong relationships with the distribution network was the only way to maintaining a strong presence in the market. The two individuals were part of the same organization, faced the same reality in the marketplace, and had similar higher order objectives, but they went about achieving them by deploying two very different mental models of sales generation.

Alternatively, mental models may be entrenched not at just the individual but at the organizational level. For example, many organizations—including several that are household names—are, or at least claim to be, committed to "innovation." There is a belief inside these organizations that innovation is the engine that drives growth and helps keep competition at bay. Of course, there is nothing wrong is pursuing innovation as a tactic or even as a sustained strategy. However, over time, innovation often turns into a standard, unmoving mental model that is deployed to address a wide class of business problems. The adoption of innovation as almost a platform for solving all business problems itself is not innovative at all. It precludes management from asking questions about the financial returns on innovation and examining whether alternative strategies unrelated to innovation might be more profitable.

These models also reside within larger professional communities. For example, the marketing community often promotes concepts such as customer centricity or long-term customer relationships as mental models or platforms to sustain revenue and margin growth over time. And finally, some business models transcend organizational and professional boundaries. For example, the current move toward evaluating all organizational activities in terms of "equity" or incremental financial value is a mental model that seems to transcend functional silos.

There is fundamentally nothing wrong in using mental models to address strategic problems. These problems tend to be complex and have many interdependent moving parts. If one starts from scratch to begin addressing each problem one might find most of them to be intractable. Mental models bring certain efficiency to the decision-making process and provide useful heuristics. They have implicit cause-and-effect relationships built inside them that help managers map out the consequences of certain actions and evaluate the quality of the outcomes. Mental models also serve as sorting devices that help managers categorize the issues in terms of their relative importance. Finally, such models provide cues for the selection of metrics that can serve as indicators of strategic progress.

However, we find that the simplicity these mental models bring to the table sometimes comes at an extremely high cost. In order to break through the constraints imposed by these models, it is important for managers to pause and think about the set of assumptions that drive their beliefs in them. In order to get started, we have come up with a set of 10 questions that every manager should ask of these models before they become entrenched in the decision-making process.

The Myth of One

We find that very often the example of one firm or one product either deliberately or accidentally becomes the torchbearer for the success or failure of a specific strategy. Managers at other firms in both related and unrelated industries then refer to this single example as an illustration of why a specific strategy in question would work in their own specific circumstances. For example, we find that managers quote the same example of an office products company when claiming the importance of moving their customers from "satisfied" to "very satisfied." In the case of this specific firm, there was a very significant difference between the repurchase intent of satisfied and very-satisfied customers. However, we have come across numerous cases where such a relationship was either not as strong or not evident at all. However, managers who believe in moving their customers to the top end of the satisfaction scale overweight their single favorite example and fail to verify whether corresponding relationships exist within their own organizational context. Other examples of what we call "the myth of one" include Apple for innovation-driven growth, Wal-Mart for the power of low prices, General Electric for diversification and multicategory branding, and Dell for direct-to-consumer distribution. While the use of these single, illustrative examples is perhaps appropriate, what we find missing is a serious attempt to map the strategic context of the examples onto one's own circumstances and an evaluation of whether similar benefits will necessarily accrue.

The Myth of Many

As the name suggests, the myth of many is the exact opposite of the myth of one but leads to similar strategic shortcomings. In this case, managers often erroneously assume that strategies that have worked for a large number of other firms will also work in their specific case. Consequently, they herd toward a common strategy that others are apparently following successfully. For example, many have boarded the outsourcing band-wagon just because everyone else was doing so, and it appeared to be the right thing to do. Similarly, many have pursued customer loyalty–driven or brand portfolio rationalization–driven strategies because a large number of others did so. Once again, what we find missing is the due diligence to examine specifically whether the same strategy that apparently worked for many others will work similarly in one's own specific circumstance and to what extent.

Locus Focus: What Does It Pick Up Versus Leave Behind?

This is what we call the vacuum cleaner (VC) question. Whether or not we acknowledge it, most mental models are not all encompassing and focus on a limited central notion. Most are seriously limited in what they can account for. For example, customer centricity promotes customer satisfaction or loyalty as the central theme around which strategy should be built. The thrust of this approach is to focus on customers' responses to the firm's offerings and reengineer the firm's strategy in order to optimize the level of satisfaction delivered to the customer. Similarly brand-centric strategies focus on brand equity as a core construct that becomes the locus of constructing strategy and evaluating its effectiveness. The planning process under this strategy is guided by building brand equity or leveraging it within existing and new markets. And the consequence of strategic choices is measured by watching and measuring brand equity and estimating its impact on the value of the firm.

However, as they are successively promoted, adopted, or implemented, these models are often assumed to be able to do more than what they are really capable of. In other words, over time the collateral beliefs that accompany simple models stretch beyond the domain of what the models are supposed to cover. For example, we often run into managers who have a mental model that price discounts from competitors should be met with price discounts in order to preserve market share. The belief is that a price response to a price challenge captures most, if not all, of the dynamics of the interaction between the rival firms. While this may be the appropriate strategy under certain circumstances, it may not be under others. However, in either case, we find that managers often fail to account for the collateral effects of their pricing decisions. They typically fail to map out how price changes might influence brand perceptions, dealer responses, funds for future product development, or employee morale. A focus on the locus of the mental model also pushes alternative sound ideas to the periphery. The locus begins to almost match the mission of the firm, and strategic choices slowly align around it, often at the detriment of alternative options.

This or Abyss

Mental models may or may not be data driven. If they are tied strongly to some core beliefs inside the organization, they tend to promote strategic inflexibility and a culture of nonverification. They devalue alternative courses of action and raise perceptions of risk from deviating from the prescribed path. For example, when managers commit to market share–based strategies, they tend to devalue all strategic options that are unrelated to an increase in market share. The likelihood that they would give up share as a core metric of importance also goes down. Similarly, those who commit to a model advocating operational efficiency devalue alternatives that may otherwise be viable and beneficial but inconsistent with the principle of efficiency.

Similarly, other firms become closely tied to the principle of innovation and a collective belief that it is the key and only driver of long-term competitiveness and profitability. Of course, the principle of innovation also brings certain cohesiveness to a firm's product strategy and may serve as a binding force among its employees. However, many firms that follow innovation as a *mantra* do not verify whether the strategy is actually as big a contributor to success as they think it is. The overarching mental model centered on innovation tends to build a culture of basing decisions on intuition rather than on verifying whether the individual and collective beliefs of the organization are true or not. The culture then closes the paths to alternative strategies, especially those that may be the polar opposite of those that the internal culture promotes. For example, the culture at innovation-driven firms does not promote imitation-driven strategies and a verification of whether innovation truly beats imitation as a product strategy.

Does the Model Have a Reverse Gear?

As we noted earlier, mental models lead to a locus focus, that is, selective attention on a few metrics that capture the spirit of the mental model. For example, customer satisfaction may capture the essence of a customer-centric mental model. However, what is also noteworthy is not only the selection of a model-specific metric but also a commitment to the direction in which to move it. In most cases, revenue-oriented metrics are always expected to move up, and cost oriented metrics are always expected to move down. While there is fundamentally nothing wrong in this approach, the focus on the metric prevents managers from asking questions about what would happen if the metric were to move in the opposite direction and whether it is appropriate to let it do so. We once came across a flourishing medical practice that diligently followed its customer satisfaction scores and had a major research firm collect the data and provide a consolidated report. However, at one point in time, it discovered that its satisfaction scores were slipping and its profitability was improving. Of course, several factors might explain the inverse correlation between satisfaction and firm profitability. However, the discovery of this unexpected relationship was troublesome because it violated the mental model around which the practice built its entire customer-centric strategy. It violated the directional premise that the way to drive profitability higher was to drive the satisfaction score *higher*.

Therefore mental models not only drive the strategic energy of organizations toward the metrics that become the locus of attention but also influence the direction in which these metrics need to be moved in order to succeed. Strategic choices that circumvent these key metrics and yet are profitable are moved off the table, and a drop in these metrics is interpreted as an indication of a failure to achieve the strategic goals.

The point is that as soon as we embrace a mental model, we embrace the metrics surrounding it; we fail to ask questions about what would happen if we were to turn them on their head. What would happen if we were to let satisfaction levels of certain stakeholders slip? Will we necessarily be worse off? What would happen if quality levels went down or brand equity was lower than what it is now? Therefore, before we embrace a mental model of strategy, we should clearly ask if it has a reverse gear. Will it ever advocate a course reversal? And if so, then does it have built-in indicators that would start flashing that a reversal is indeed warranted? Or will it be left to us as individual decision makers to figure out when we should abandon course and look for alternatives? And if so, then will it be too late by the time such a discovery is made?

Is the Model Forward Prescriptive or Backward Diagnostic?

At a very fundamental level, there are two ways of building mental models of cause and effect. We can build them from left to right—that is, from the cause to the effect, something we refer to as forward prescriptive. Or we can build them from right to left, that is, from effect to causes, something that we refer to as backward diagnostic. While both approaches should ultimately link causes and effects, a natural question to ask is whether there would be a difference between the two. One can certainly argue that mathematically speaking, the forward prescriptive models and backward diagnostic models should converge. Further, would the data not tell the same story whether we think one way or another? Perhaps they would. However, we find that the two approaches lead to a vastly different set of questions that managers ask themselves and very different sets of places where they seek answers.

Generally, we find that forward prescriptive models are the norm as far as mental models go. Managers tend to believe that certain paths will lead to successful outcomes and plot strategies in order to move forward in that direction. Very often, these paths come from a silo-based perspective, where managers attempt to link the metrics within their silos to the metrics of overall firm performance. For instance, marketers might try to show the relationship between measures such as customer satisfaction and customer retention with measures of corporate profitability. Similarly, human resource managers might attempt to demonstrate the positive relationship between measures of employee engagement and overall firm profitability. Forward prescriptive models tend to have built-in intermediate markers that are assumed to be measures of success. Organizational effort then focuses on two things. The first is to invest in initiatives that are consistent with the model that will drive the levels of the intermediate markers to an acceptable level. And the second is to examine whether achieving these desired levels has the expected effect on the final outcome of interest, such as financial performance. The following are typical sets of questions that managers working with some common forward prescriptive models will ask themselves:

Brand Equity–Based Forward Prescriptive Model
1. Do our brands have high or low equity at this moment?
2. How do we build equity in our brands?
3. Does increasing brand equity increase our market share, pricing power, and profits?

Customer Satisfaction–Based Forward Prescriptive Model
1. How satisfied are our customers with our products and services?
2. What can we do to increase customer satisfaction?
3. Does increasing customer satisfaction increase our market share, pricing power, and profits?

A similar set of questions is put together for other forward prescriptive models that are built around customer loyalty, operational efficiency, competence, employee orientation, and other similar paradigms. What is noteworthy is that these paradigms rest on a key intermediate metric such as equity or customer satisfaction that is the focus of the entire forward-based thinking. Connections are then made from organizational initiatives to this metric and now increasingly from the metric to its consequences.

Backward diagnostic models start from the right-hand side and work their way to the left-hand side through flexible paths. Our experience is that these models are not as popular as their forward prescriptive counterparts, in part because they require a deviation from silo-based decision making. Their implementation is not tied to achieving targeted levels on preset metrics. Under this paradigm, one starts from looking at the most effective driver of the ultimate or terminal performance and the metrics that capture these drivers. The next steps then successively unfold these drivers to their simplest and most disaggregate form. This disaggregate set of actions constitutes the portfolio that would be expected to drive the ultimate financial performance. The following types of questions would be on the table using a backward diagnostic approach:

1. What are the drivers of margins in the business?
2. What is the relationship between market share and gross margins?
3. What are the drivers of market share across segments?
4. Should market share be increased across all segments or should certain segments be vacated?
5. What is the relationship between product design and unit prices and market share and margins?

As one will notice, no single paradigm sets the bounds for the series of questions, and the exploration can lead to very different sets of answers and solutions depending on what the circumstances are and what the data reveal. There are no universal metrics whose value needs to be maximized as a matter of rule. On the contrary, the process of discovering the appropriate metrics moves in a reverse direction, guided by the likely impact that they would have on the downstream measures of interest. In other words, if margin is a downstream metric of interest, then the backward diagnostic approach is completely flexible with regard to discovering the upstream metrics that drive margins. They might include high market share and low prices or vice versa. To that extent, the backward diagnostic approach relies on a data-driven discovery process to determine both the key metrics and the direction in which to drive them.

Overall, when one executes strategy, it might be worthwhile to explicitly ask whether one's mental model is forward prescriptive or backward diagnostic. A mere consciousness of the type of model one is working under will help realize the extent of its flexibility and its ability to discover paths to profitability.

Data Analysis and Data Generation Process

This is perhaps a subtle issue but a good analysis of data can at best provide information about the process that led to the generation of the data itself. If a specific data generation process did not exist then an analysis of the data will provide no clues about the process. For example, consider a situation where a single company or a pool of companies invests in *raising* customer loyalty levels. In other words, there is no effort or resource expended in *reducing* loyalty from the current levels or in exploring other options to manage the customer base. Imagine that at some later point an analysis is done to assess whether the strategic choice to try to increase customer loyalty is paying off in financial terms. Now what is important to note is that this analysis, if appropriately conducted, can only tell us whether an *increase* in loyalty resulted in any change in the marketplace or financial performance of the firm. It will not be able to address issues pertaining to what would have happened if the firm or firms had chosen to *reduce* loyalty and chosen another strategic path.

Said differently, the data analysis can only inform us about the data generating process. If there is no attempt to choose strategic options that would generate the data relating to those options, one will not be able to learn whether the options that were not chosen would have resulted in outcomes that would have been better or worse than those that were chosen. Therefore, if a firm or a group of firms chooses the path on increased customer loyalty, a subsequent analysis of the data will not be able to uncover whether an alternative path, such as changing the wages of the frontline workers would have resulted in a better or worse outcome. Overall, a firm can discover the links between the chosen paths and observed outcomes but not those between foregone paths and possible outcomes.

Mental models restrict strategic choices to those that make intuitive sense and prevent the discovery of alternative routes to firm profitability. They prevent experimentation with novel paths and tie the firm down to only those that seem to be consistent with the model. Consequently, even under the best case scenario, the firm learns about whether the model-consistent path is worthwhile or not. It fails to gather the information necessary to compare model-consistent and model-inconsistent paths to judge which one would be superior. For example, if a firm follows an innovation-centric mental model and makes choices that are broadly consistent with it, then it may never discover the power of imitation-based strategies.

Objectives Versus Constraints

Mental models in some sense are statements of objectives and constraints. The objectives are set in terms of final or intermediate targets, and constraints result from either limited resources or the inability to meet the most desirable level of the objective even if reasonable resources were available. For example, a firm can have an *intermediate* objective, such as achieving greater than 95% satisfaction among current customers. Or it could have a *terminal* objective such as achieving the largest market share in a chosen product market within a specified period of time. It could also have a much more abstract objective such as sustainable development or balancing the interests of the internal and external stakeholders.

Strategic flag posts are intermediate markers or targets that help organizations test and diagnose the progress being made along the chosen path. Certain mental models directly lend themselves to a construct identification, measurement, and tracking system while others do not. For example, it is relatively easy to build flag posts around customer centricity–based models and measure and track customer responses to the organization's own initiatives and competitive activity. On the other hand, it is relatively difficult to set flag posts around an innovation-centric mental model. It is relatively difficult to define innovativeness, classify it, measure and track it, and connect it to firm success. One of the most common challenges for companies seeking growth through innovation is that the metrics that these companies use to measure innovation can actually lead companies in the wrong direction. For example, if managers are rewarded on the percentage of revenues from new products—a terminal flag post—a brand manager might be highly tempted to promote a new incrementally innovative product that might actually cannibalize an existing firm offering, instead of investing in a longer gestation innovative product that can provide greater long-term incremental revenue to the organization. Similarly, a focus on inputs rather than outputs of an innovation, can lead a firm to focus on research and development (R&D) investments rather than the deliverables achieved from such investments. Some common examples are Ford and IBM that have huge R&D budgets and a large number of patents respectively, without corresponding market leadership.[1]

The constraints could also be stipulated along multiple dimensions. There could be financial constraints such as those imposed by limited budgets or threshold levels of returns required on investments. There may be constraints on capabilities, such as those arising out of the capacity of the workforce and the ability to hire qualified people in the right numbers at the right time. Constraints may also result from the legacy of the organization. For example, the existing portfolio of brands held by the company may limit its flexibility in maneuvering in the product-market space. And certain choices, although feasible and maybe desirable in their own right, may be inconsistent with the overall strategy of the company. For instance, opportunities at the lower end of a market may conflict with the overall company strategy of focusing on higher tiers and may therefore be constraints.

Is the Model Synchronous With the Adoption Cycle?

Much like fashion, models of strategy go through cycles. For example, the current model of manufacturing and back office operations is entrenched in outsourcing to low-cost countries. This model, and many others that precede it, emanated from one business or sector and then cascaded across the landscape to touch many firms or sectors of the economy. Those who are early to adopt these trends are likely to reap a differential advantage over their competitors. However, others who are at the tail end of the cycle risk being entrapped in a model that belongs to a previous generation of business practice and may not offer any differential advantage. If this is done repeatedly, in that a model is adopted after it becomes popular and widespread, then one may be trapped in a cycle where the trend that gets adopted is the one that is about to perish. Therefore, it is important to examine whether or not the mental model one plans to adopt is synchronous with model cycles. It is important to appreciate the peaks and valleys tied to the usefulness and appropriateness of these models and be flexible enough to adopt the next paradigm when it becomes relevant.

Half-Life of the Model

As we stated earlier, the business landscape evolves and changes over time, and strategic models that may be used to succeed under these changing circumstances need to keep up with the direction and pace of change. We propose that it might be useful to clearly ask the question as to what is the half-life of the mental model that is currently in use. What is the time frame over which the utility of the model reduces? The longer the half-life, the greater will be the likelihood that the model can help guide decision making for a longer period.

A focus on a specific mental model often leads to the ignorance of key marketplace issues, which can eventually lead to lost market share and missed fortunes for an organization. The Japanese quality movement teaches us a lesson here, where the focus on quality has led to the virtual loss of the dynamic random access memory (DRAM) chip industry to Korean firms. Within the Japanese way of thinking, there is strong acceptance of a positive relationship between quality and business success. Nowhere is this belief more obvious than in the automobile industry, a very visible user of modern quality improvement technology. Quality, especially reliability, of Japanese automobiles if often cited as the primary reason for their global dominance. However, there is other evidence that suggests an emphasis on quality may not always result in equivalent benefits in other industries. A recent study found an inverse relationship between the number of International Organization for Standardization (ISO) certifications and the number of original patents, concluding that too much focus on incremental process improvements crowds out exploratory innovations that can lead to more patents. Similarly, recent management literature suggests that tools of quality improvement, such as Six Sigma, are not suited to innovation. The reason is that tools such as Six Sigma lead to a culture of quality improvement and cost reduction, which conflicts with the freethinking and risk-taking culture required for new idea generation.

The global market share of Japanese DRAM producers dropped precipitously from as high as 80% in 1989 to 10% in 2004. The Japanese had historically dominated the industry with a focus on quality products that served the needs of mainframe computers. They differentiated their products through reliable and durable chips, aiming for 25 years' durability, which served the mainframe market very well. Japanese engineers were rewarded for incremental improvements they made to the quality of the products, which added more production and testing steps and higher manufacturing costs to the overall process. In the early and mid-1990s, the market demand for DRAM saw a substantial shift from mainframe to PCs, and then to consumer products such as DVD players and cameras. This introduced significant changes to the product requirements, and speed and cost became relatively more important. This is when the Korean manufacturers entered the market, without any legacy from the mainframe days. Firms such as Samsung designed products like the

128Mbit DRAM in 2000 and targeted it at vendors of low-priced computers and servers. The Japanese were not prepared for these changes in
the marketplace and withdrew from the competitive landscape. Korean
manufacturers like Samsung were able to capitalize on their initial success
through aggressive capital investments and by continuing to focus on the
changing needs of the users.[2]

Avoiding the Trap

Managers often make decisions on the basis of intuition that brings comfort and efficiency to a legacy-based decision process. They often fail to
bring in facts to validate decisions, leading to a high hidden cost of intuition. We suggest that these managers should pause and ask questions of
their mental models in order to test the relevance and appropriateness of
their intuition. Otherwise, a lack of continuous verification of mental
models can lead to a destructive cycle that can ultimately trap organizations into suboptimal and sometimes even disastrous decision making.

CHAPTER 4

Paradigm Cycles and Strategy Prisons

Strategic prisons are overarching mental models that become sweeping guiding principles for making strategic and tactical decisions under a broad range of circumstances and that ultimately trap organizations. They are pieces of popular intuition that eventually turn into well-accepted truisms and get entrenched into the belief systems of decision makers. For example, how many of us will argue against the principles of differentiation, competency, customer satisfaction, diversification, or many such well-accepted truisms? Of course, they may well be important considerations when making key strategic choices in many domains and may often be true. After all, they have emerged from the collective experiences and wisdom of academics, researchers, managers, entrepreneurs, and consultants. Moreover, when put together, they may collectively constitute a comprehensive tool kit that can be employed in a diverse set of situations using just the power of analogy. However, these tools may have limitations and may not be as universally applicable as their proponents would like to believe.

For example, take the principle of customer focus that is at the core of many decisions and guides a number of processes inside an organization. Many firms employ the voice of the customer to aid in product design and select a feature set that is most preferred by a sample of customers who participate in the research process. Others work to optimize their in-store customer experiences that presumably drive sales. Still others track postpurchase customer satisfaction and direct strategy to maintain it at a reasonably high level. Taken together, customer focus becomes a mental model in these organizations that drives decision making from prepurchase product design to selling and postsale customer management.

Certainly, there is absolutely nothing wrong in being customer focused and using the principle to guide a variety of decisions and business processes. If one looks, one can always find evidence for the positive effects of customer-focused choices on business performance. However, there are three potential dangers that such a singular approach to strategy expose a firm to. First, as the guiding principle embeds itself in the decision-making process, it suppresses the verification process. Over time, managers do not feel the need to examine whether and to what extent following such an overarching principle is indeed driving firm performance. Second, being wedded to one principle limits the process of discovering alternative principles that are inconsistent with the current one, even though they might lead to superior performance. And finally, an attachment to one principle influences the culture of the organization and coerces nonbelievers to constrain their voices.

For example, in a case referenced in chapter 3, an extremely successful medical practice discovered that while its customer satisfaction scores were decreasing over time, its profitability was increasing. The evidence was contrary to the mental model around which the practice was built. Now if the practice had chosen to continue with its current mental model, it would have increased its investments in its customer management program, and the results may not have been favorable. However, it chose to challenge its model and followed the data to wherever it led. Ultimately, they discovered that the variable causing the discrepancy between the trends in the satisfaction scores and firm profits was the size of the facility or customer processing capacity that was leading to excessive waiting times. Over time, an increase in capacity utilization led profits to go higher but patient satisfaction to decline. The solution to the problem did not lie in traditional satisfaction enhancement programs but in capacity investment.

The Formation of Strategic Prisons

How do these strategy prisons form and what prevents either individuals or organizations from recognizing that they are inside one (Figure 4.1)? We believe that the formation of prisons follows a process that starts with a simple idea or what we call a metathought and ends up with collective entrenchment or entrapment in a prison. The initial core idea leads to the

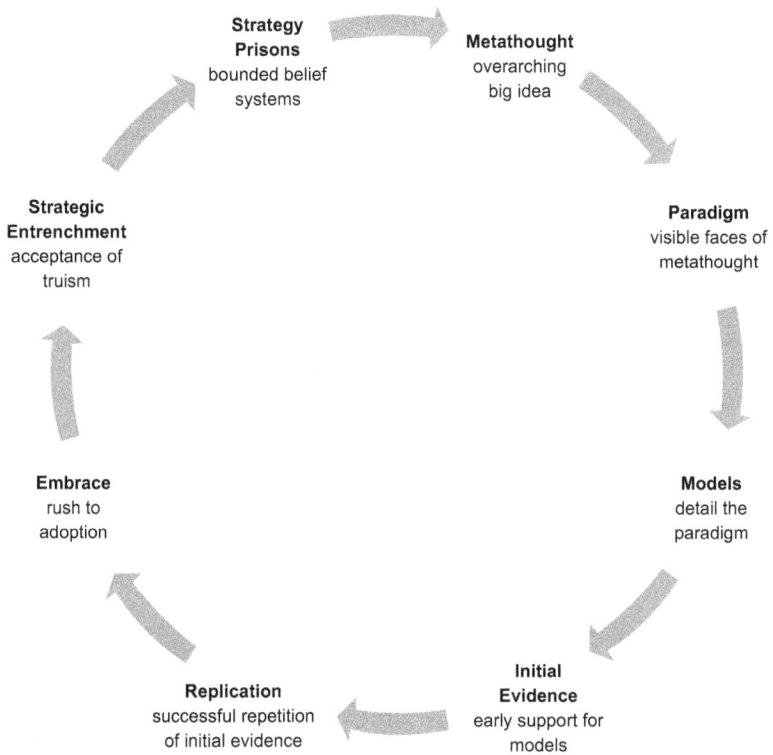

Figure 4.1. Paradigm cycles.

articulation of a paradigm and a set of models within it. Over time, these models feed upon themselves, and their repeated replication reinforces their utility and shackles the strategists. This "prison term" often continues despite evidence to the contrary until a disruptive model emerges that challenges the conventional wisdom and opens up a new path to optimal long-term business performance. Of course, as always, the new model bears the same risk as the previous one in that it can start a new wave of followers who may finally get trapped in the new prison. In other words, strategic mental models tend to follow a pattern that might look like fashion cycles where people collectively herd toward the latest and greatest and then migrate over to the next generation whenever it arrives only to be collectively trapped there until the alternative arrives.

   An example of such entrapment can be traced back to more than four decades ago. As they strived to achieve sustainable competitive advantage, many organizations embraced the paradigm of customer centricity (the metathought). Among the many models that came forth to achieve such centricity, the measurement of customer experience feedback through customer satisfaction and loyalty programs took center stage. In one of the earliest published texts on the topic in the mid-1960s, a unidimensional measure of "overall satisfaction" was proposed. As initial evidence and subsequent replication found increasing support for the notion, researchers and practitioners embraced the idea. Subsequently, other follow-up evidence pointed to the need for a more expansive and multidimensional measurement of customer experience. This led to the development of many alternate models, each of which found its own group of believers. It is only now that the concept seems to have come full circle with challenges being raised to the paradigm of customer centricity, the construct of customer satisfaction, and the measurement system that accompanies it.

How Paradigm Cycles Work

Metathought: The Initial Spark

A metathought is an overarching big idea that has the potential to influence business practice across decision domains or across firms or potentially both. It may not necessarily be a completely new or untested idea but it is popularized by a champion at a point in time and catches the fancy of many. For example, a metathought could be that one should create new and uncontested markets and get out of the way of competitors rather than fight with them for a share of an existing market. Now if the status quo were that most firms were actually engaged in a market share battle and collectively followed the same mind-set, then the new idea would be what we would call a metathought. An idea such as this would have the potential to influence organizations in many ways and across a variety of functional domains. For example, an organization that would follow the metathought will have to make a fundamental change in how it defines markets and how it would change its focus to creating new ones. It will also have to think differently regarding what competition means and why it might not be prudent to go head-to-head against it. The metathought will change the focus of its product development initiatives to market creation and away from share extraction. Finally, the metrics that it would use to evaluate the product development process, its marketplace performance, its financial performance, and the overall organizational risk will change. The new set of metrics may bear little resemblance to those that were used in the past or are currently used by others in related business sectors.

Similarly, another metathought could be that a customer's ability to pay may be uncorrelated with an organization's ability to profit. In other words, the most profitable customers may not be the ones who have the greatest individual earning power but are few in numbers—rather those with lower individual purchasing power but greater collective strength. If this metathought is adopted, then it has the power to change the market selection process and the mechanisms the organization employs to evaluate market attractiveness and to do an opportunity analysis. Organizations who follow the metathought would then think differently about product development, pricing formats, package sizes, distribution systems, and customer retention. In other words, the single metathought would change a lot of what the organization would do and how it would do it.

Yet another metathought could be that an organization should not do many things but focus on just one or a few areas of strength. The adoption of this premise will redirect an organization's efforts away from diversification and a portfolio-based approach toward concentration and focus areas. This concentration could be in terms of resource allocation, skill building, market selection, or product policy. On the other hand, a somewhat different metathought could be that organizations can mitigate their business risk by doing many unrelated things. Such a thought would direct organizational energies in the exact opposite direction where coverage might become important, as would diversity of skill set and a broadening of the product line and a wider selection of markets. One can easily see that the two metathoughts would give rise to very different strategic directions that would have an impact on decision making at all levels from resource allocation to product positioning.

A metathought can also arise at a domain specific level. For example, an idea could be that if you treat your employees well they in turn will treat the customers well. An adoption of this metathought would direct much of the organizational energy toward fine-tuning its people management policies and ensuring that its employees are treated well and are cared for. It would unleash an employee-centered culture with the central premise being that satisfied employees will automatically satisfy the customer base.

Finally, another example of a domain-specific metathought would be the notion that a customer is only as good as the incremental cash flow that he or she can bring to the organization in the future. The adoption of this metathought would change the firm's customer relationship strategies from backward looking to forward looking. It would directly evaluate customers in terms of their net financial value and would almost automatically impose a segmentation system where valuable customers are segregated from less valuable ones. And finally, it would direct resources toward customers who are valuable and away from those who are not. One such potential manifestation of resource allocation is witnessed in organizations that measure the worth of their customers in terms of not only the revenue the firm currently gets from them but also the incremental potential that is available. Such a perspective has heightened the interest in measures such as "share of wallet" that allow firms to juxtapose their current earnings from individual customers against the total category spend of these customers. With such an understanding, two customers with, say, a thousand dollars' worth of revenue could be treated very differently if one of these customers allocates a 100% share to the firm compared to only 5% share allocated by the second customer. The firm can clearly see much larger incremental sales potential for the second customer, whereas without this perspective, both customers might have been treated identically.

Paradigm: Building the Framework

Paradigms are the visible or manifest faces of metathoughts and represent its key tenets to a wide audience (Figure 4.1). They might start as labels and may ultimately become the metaphorical version of the underlying metathought and represent the collection of practices under it.

For example, Blue Ocean Strategy is the paradigmatic version of the fact that one should create uncontested markets. In this case, red oceans metaphorically represent the battle among competitors within an existing market space and blue oceans represent the serene, separated, uncontested market that one is advised to create. The metaphor gives meaning to the metathought of creating uncontested markets and almost provides an automatic logic to it. Individual decisions and collective strategies get organized as blue ocean strategies. The paradigm also becomes the commonly accepted verbalization of the underlying metathought, and strategists start using it as a lens to view whether a chosen set of actions are consistent with the metathought or not.

Serving people at the bottom of the pyramid is the paradigm that postulates that firms can build a profitable business by focusing on those who have the least ability to pay. It captures the essence of the metathought that it might not always be wise to chase those customers who might individually be the most profitable. It points to the collective power of those at the bottom of the pyramid and exhorts firms to change their product design, pricing formats, and business models to generate adequate returns from what would conventionally be considered an unprofitable segment. Recent announcements in the computing sector provide a testament to this changing orientation. In May 2008, Microsoft came up with an innovative piece of software, FlexGo, which keeps machines from working unless users type in a number from a prepaid card. After a certain number of hours, the computer becomes the property of the consumer. The intent is to minimize the up-front payment in developing countries, and instead charge such consumers some amount up front, and then the remaining over time. Similarly, Intel launched the "Community PC" in March 2008. This machine is targeted at rural Indians, who can share a machine or might want to share it with others in the family and community. The PC costs about $550, has a filter to keep out the dust, can run on a car battery during blackouts, and has a single-button recovery system in the event of a crash. At the same time, Intel introduced a $250–$350 miniaturized desktop, and Mexican officials have already ordered 400,000 of these for delivery.

Similarly, the notion of core competence is the paradigmatic version of the metathought that one should do a few things well and become better at those over time. The core competence label becomes the carrier of the metathought and provides face validity to it. The converse is the paradigm of diversification, which carries the message that it is unwise to put all of one's eggs in one basket. And finally, the customer equity paradigm is the carrier of the metathought that a customer should be valued in terms of the future discounted cash flow that it is able to generate for the firm. Consequently, a firm should divert greater incremental resources to those customers who are more profitable and away from those who are not.

Models: Detailing the Paradigm

The acceptance of a paradigm often leads to models that delineate the process by which the paradigm is implemented and tested (Figure 4.1). For example, the customer equity paradigm has generated a number of models in both the conceptual and empirical domains. These models serve several interrelated purposes. First, they help finesse the key constructs that are central to the paradigm. They also help define what customer equity really means and what it does not. And finally, they also help separate the paradigm from those that are seemingly closely related with it, such as the customer loyalty paradigm or the brand equity paradigm.

Models also help answer questions that establish the domain or the outer bounds of the paradigm. For example, they will help delineate whether the notion of customer equity relates to only the current customers of the firm or extends to future potential customers as well. Does it focus on the current portfolio of products or take into account product additions and deletions as well? How does one use data to estimate the value of equity and then incorporate it into strategic decisions? Can the construct help answer strategic decisions at a firm level or tactical decisions at a product-market level?

Finally, conceptual models are translated into quantitative or statistical models. These translations help in developing a measurement system for sizing up the key constructs embedded in the paradigm. In addition, they help in identifying the upstream antecedents of these constructs and establish a system for measuring their downstream impact. To that extent, these models facilitate the translation of the paradigm into a form that can be implemented with data and help establish a system to evaluate the goodness of the implementation.

Initial Evidence: The Proof of the Pudding

Initial evidence that is consistent with their basic tenets is critical for the survival of new paradigms (Figure 4.1). This evidence could be qualitative and anecdotal or quantitative and statistical. For example, the early support could come from case studies that show in very general terms that following the paradigm led to superior business results. For instance, Cirque du Soleil is often cited as an example of an organization that witnessed tremendous growth using the Blue Ocean Strategy. Blue Ocean here refers to untapped market space with the potential for high and profitable growth. In contrast, Red Oceans describe marketplaces with intense competition. What Cirque du Soleil did was not compete against established competitors, such as Ringling Brothers and Barnum and Bailey, for market share of the kids' audience, which was already drawn to other forms of digital entertainment. Instead of winning customers from the already declining circus industry, it created a new market space that made the competition irrelevant. It appealed to a very new demographic comprising adults and corporate clients that were willing to pay much higher prices for a great entertainment experience. Compelling initial evidence, such as this, provides the required face validity for a paradigm and helps generate broad-based support.

Replication: It Works Every Time

Once the initial evidence is in place, there is an urge among many to adopt the paradigm. In some cases, the replication might be successful while in others it might not be. However, stories of successful replications start coming forth and bolster the case for the paradigm. The collection of positive implementations becomes a resounding endorsement, and the paradigm is seen as more than just a temporary success. The failures to replicate tend not to become equally powerful stories and do not get an equal share of voice. Consequently, the landscape becomes dotted with stories of success, and the paradigm is thought to be more generalizable that what it actually might be.

Embrace: The Herding Begins

Once the stories of successful replication surface, the rush to adoption begins. Suddenly everyone wants to be either customer centric or relationship oriented. Along the same lines, some limited success stories associated with the "net promoter score" as a metric of customer centricity has led to an adoption of the same, without verification of the tenets of the approach and its applicability to the industry, the company, or the research objectives. Many rush to find blue oceans or to serve the bottom of the pyramid, after successful case studies such as Cirque du Soleil discussed earlier. Others converge toward building an employee-centered culture or serve the customers with the greatest lifetime values or with the greatest cost efficiency. For example, Comfort Inn and Motel 6 have positioned themselves as low-cost alternatives to other hospitality brands such as Holiday Inn and Ramada Inn. Enterprise Rent-a-Car is a low-cost alternative to Hertz and Avis. Similarly, on the other end of the spectrum of the hospitality industry, hotel brands such as Marriott and Ritz Carlton take pride in their employee-centric cultures. At Ritz, the corporate motto is "We are ladies and gentlemen serving ladies and gentlemen," and these organizations place great emphasis on employee welfare and engagement, and in turn, provide great customer experiences. Still others want to rationalize their brand portfolios and build the highest possible brand equity. There is, of course, nothing wrong in following any of these approaches and each has its own merit. However, once a group of players herds toward the same strategic mind-set, it tends to follow and mimic each other's approaches and converges toward the same playbook. However, more importantly, while operating within a given strategic paradigm, the entire group suppresses the need for verifying the extent to which it is applicable to its own unique set of circumstances, and misses the opportunity to discover better and more appropriate pathways toward profitable business performance.

Entrenchment: Blocking the Exits

Not surprisingly, herding ultimately leads to strategic entrenchment (Figure 4.1). Organizations become "psychologically" wedded to the paradigm and accept it as one of the few truisms that guide their fate. Executives from many firms have shared such stories in the past. Employees at Nordstrom often cite an instance where the sales representative took back a customer's 2-year-old blouse with no questions asked. Likewise, a frequently told story at UPS tells of an employee who, without authorization, ordered an extra Boeing 737 to ensure timely delivery of a load of Christmas packages that had been left behind in the holiday rush. As the story goes, instead of punishing the employee, UPS rewarded his initiative to manifest company support and commitment to worker empowerment and customer service. Similarly, Averitt Express uses the slogan

"Our driving force is people" to communicate its commitment to treating employees and customers well. Google is wedded to the idea of bottom-up idea generation and strongly encourages employees at all levels of the organization to bring forth their ideas. This process is facilitated by an "ideas mailing list" that allows all employees to post their idea proposals. Such ideas are then short-listed for further review and development. 3M is known for its innovative ideas and emphasis on intrapreneurship, that is, entrepreneurship within the organization. The organizational structure at 3M is such that central research and development (R&D) researchers find and collaborate with business units that best understand the market for a new product. Executives at 3M have realized that once scientists are able to get their products from the lab to the market, they get hooked on the process. The R&D function is consequently streamlined for researchers excited about commercializing their research. This has led to a significant reduction in the product development life cycle as well as more efficient R&D spending that has churned out some of the most exciting new products within the world of nanotechnology, such as ultrabright cell phone displays, natural-looking dental fillings, and superconductive power cables.

As is obvious from such anecdotes, entrenchment is not without its benefits. It helps spread a core operating principle throughout the organization and serves as a control mechanism. For example, if an organization is wedded to customer satisfaction, then the entrenchment of the paradigm ensures that most, if not all, employees behave in a manner that is consistent with satisfying the customer. On the other hand, if an organization is wedded to an entrepreneurship culture, then it promotes such behavior among its employees, and the reward systems evolve to compensate them for exhibiting risk-taking behavior.

Entrenchment also serves to stabilize organizations and helps them find a course and stay the course for an extended period. For example, if an organization is built around the innovation paradigm, it is likely to continue on a path of producing novel products, services, or technologies for an extended period and not waver from that path every now and then. It also helps organizations weather storms that come from failures along the way. In the absence of entrenched paradigms, organizations may be changing course at a rate that might not be in their best long-term interest.

However, entrenchment closes doors to discovery and suppresses the emergence of alternative pathways to progress and performance. Sometimes the entrenchment is embedded inside what may be called the culture of the organization and deviations from it are either rare or not encouraged. One very often cited example is that of Apple, which today is arguably the most innovative company in its industry but for a long period was not the most financially successful. During this period of Apple's history, skeptics had questioned if creation for the sake of creation is short sighted. However, innovation benefits an organization only if it generates cash to cover the cost of innovations and to reward the shareholders. For example, analysts often argue that Apple's decision to not license its operating system in the 1970s precluded it from capturing a large share of the home PC market in its early years. The same analysts argued that Apple could have corrected the situation by capitalizing on its early lead in the $12 billion education market for PCs, which might have gotten Apple another way to enter the home PC market. Instead, Apple failed to develop an aggressive sales force, ceding its position to competitors, including some lesser known brand names such as Acer and Legend, both of which specialized in manufacturing clones of more popular PCs at the lowest possible cost. Industry observers believed that Apple focused on developing "cool" products, without an adequate emphasis on profit generation. As a result, as soon as Apple got a new product to the market, it was ready to work on the next big invention, leaving the monotony of sales and strategic partnerships to competitors. For a long time, its infatuation with R&D did not necessarily translate into equivalent business success.[1] In more recent product introductions however, such as the iPod, the iPhone, and the iPad, Apple has had more business success by paying attention to the downstream commercial aspects of these innovative offerings.

The Strategy Prison Forms: Bounded Thinking

We use the term "strategy prison" as a metaphor to represent the outer boundaries that individual managers or organizations as a whole build around their belief system. The prison affects their world view and strongly influences their perception of what works in their business and what does not. As they become trapped in the prison, they tend to follow the norms that are consistent with it and ignore or at least suppress ideas and processes that are contrarian to it.

One of the reasons why managers and executives end up in strategy prisons is because they fail to ask the right questions of their mental models, such as those asked in the previous chapter, and challenge the applicability of these models to all situations and under all circumstances. As a result, these models become an integral part of their strategic intuition and guide their decisions across a wide range of domains over extended periods. Ultimately, these executives get wedded to their mental models, claim public belief in them in front of external and internal stakeholders, and discount all reasonable challenges to them.

Being inside a strategy prison has several consequences. The first is structural in that an entrenchment within a belief system tends to limit the number of levers that the organization pulls or is willing to pull in order to move the business forward and take it to new heights. This is especially evident when the organization runs into serious headwinds. The response to a set of adverse circumstances is constructed using the same limited set of levers that the organization uses on a routine basis. Time after time, we find that when faced with adverse circumstances, cost cutting is an often resorted approach for overcoming the hurdles being faced by the organization. Often times, there is little or no consideration of the longer term impacts of such cost-cutting measures, some of which might be counter to organizational success.

The second consequence of being trapped in a strategy prison is that entrenchment defines the personality or the collective psychology of an organization. The levers that are pulled by the senior leadership tend to dictate internal processes and result in an alignment of the people within the organization along the direction in which the levers are pulled. For example, an organization that is efficiency driven will tend to promote cost consciousness at all levels and across all functional domains. On the other hand, a customer satisfaction–driven organization might lead to a service mind-set among its people. The net result is that it is not just the executive leadership or the senior management that is trapped inside its strategy prison; the rest of the organization is held captive as well.

The third consequence is that the performance measurement system, whether at the individual level or the organizational level, converges toward the current paradigm under which the organization operates.

While it appears that this should always be the case, the systems become rigid as the organization becomes entrenched in the paradigm. The rigidity reduces the flexibility to discover new strategic options and at best allows the organization to optimize locally around its current practices. And more importantly, the rigidity tends to obviate the need to continuously verify whether the paradigm is indeed driving the financial results or the bottom line of the organization. As a result, even if the organization has the information and the data to test the continuing applicability of the paradigm to their business, it tends not to do it. A very common example that we have discovered has been the euphoria associated with improvements in customer satisfaction and loyalty scores, typically reported by customers in surveys sponsored by various organizations to gauge their level of health in the marketplace. While an improvement in these scores seems an appropriate aspiration, it often leads to adverse outcomes. For example, if the most profitable customers of the firm, who are often the ones with the highest expectations and therefore likely to be least satisfied, exit and are no longer required to take satisfaction surveys, the satisfaction scores may go up at the expense of profitability. Thus the firm could be lauding itself for eroding its profitability, without ever recognizing it, even though it might very well have the data to investigate this detrimental relationship.

In the next few chapters, we will outline how a flexible, data-driven, verification-based mind-set provides an escape route from the strategy prison and has the potential to enable organizations to discover new pathways toward their strategic goals. We will also describe a methodology called linkage analysis that is a powerful tool to discover the causal and structural relationships between the levers that an organization pulls and the results that it ultimately receives. Our belief is that an adoption of the linkage mind-set and the methodology will help most organizations better channel their resources and discover new possibilities toward attaining superior, long-term profitability.

PART II

Decision Equity

CHAPTER 5

The Ultimate Management Metric?

What Is Decision Equity?

While we can discuss the notion of decision equity at many levels, let us begin with a simple definition that will capture its essence. At a fundamental level, we define decision equity as the net present value of the direct and indirect cash flows associated with revenue and margin increments or cost savings that result from the implementation of a strategic decision. In other words, the metric of decision equity captures the long-term financial consequences associated with the identification, selection, and implementation of a higher order strategic choice versus the status quo or an alternate option. One can see that the computational foundations of the concept draw upon the same common principles of financial valuation that several other strategic metrics including customer equity, brand equity, and stock prices draw from. However, as we argue in the remainder of this chapter and the rest of the book, the power of decision equity lies not necessarily in its computation but in its deployment in making strategic choices, understanding their consequences, and estimating their financial impact.

A Case Study

A case study that involves a leading credit card issuer operating in both the United States and various other parts of the world illustrates the concept of decision equity. The company wanted to identify ways to build stronger relationships with its credit card holders, in order to foster more favorable customer behavior, such as greater card usage, without an increased risk of defaults and bad loans. In order to meet this goal of greater customer centricity but with limited default rates, the firm formulated a research program. As the program unfolded, the firm did not limit itself to finding a solution within any specific, existing paradigm, such as product enhancement, that would improve card features and enhance perceptions of quality. Instead, it encouraged a paradigm-free discussion, not leaving any strategic options off the table.

Unlike in paradigm-driven discussions, this process generated a wide variety of often-unrelated strategic options with very different downstream consequences. The short-listed ones included the traditional product-centric options such as making changes to card features and including customized designs and a cash back bonus. A completely different strategic direction that focused on enhanced service was also on the table. This option envisaged the introduction of completely new services such as travel assistance and insurance offerings. A third option was a customer-specific reward and penalty system that included waiver of occasional late fees for heavy and responsible cardholders. A fourth option was to make changes in advertising and promotional messages with a view of modifying the brand's positioning. A fifth option was to review the processes and employee engagement levels at the company's call centers in order to improve the service resolution experience.

What is noteworthy is that, even with a simple and common overall goal, a paradigm-free approach generated a superset of actionable options that was far greater that what would have been possible with narrower mental models focused on product, or service, or brand, or employees. Instead, every conceivable solution was given fair consideration to assess its viability during the initial stage of the research program. While deliberating on these alternate and not mutually exclusive solutions, it also became apparent very early on that the research would need to span across multiple organization silos to unveil the pathways to achieving the terminal business objective of favorable enhanced card usage among the current customers.

In the next stage, the research team followed multiple routes to estimate the likely financial impact of each alternative course of action. It delved into the operations of the call centers and critically reviewed the employee practices that were under the aegis of the human resource function. It also reviewed the marketing plans and customer loyalty practices within the organization. It dug deep into the financial and accounting data pertaining to customer behavior. It talked at length with the team responsible for designing and reviewing card features and policies. And finally, it held extensive discussions with innovation teams tasked with introduction of new services to enhance revenues for the organization.

Based on these widely different and often unrelated explorations, the consideration set of potential strategic options was narrowed down. The next step was to examine the *linkages* across the various decision domains using the available data. These linkages constituted the cause-and-effect chains tied to each specific decision. For instance, one solution that was tested involved the decision to modify the processes at the customer call centers. In order to estimate the effects of the action, linkages were developed first between the levels of employee engagement within a call center environment and the employee ability to resolve customer issues effectively and efficiently. Simultaneously, the links between efficient resolution of customer problems and customer loyalty and between loyalty and subsequent customer usage of the card were examined. The short-term and long-term equity associated with a decision to change the policy to enhance call center employee engagement was then estimated on the basis of the strength of this sequence of linkages (Figure 5.1). While the short

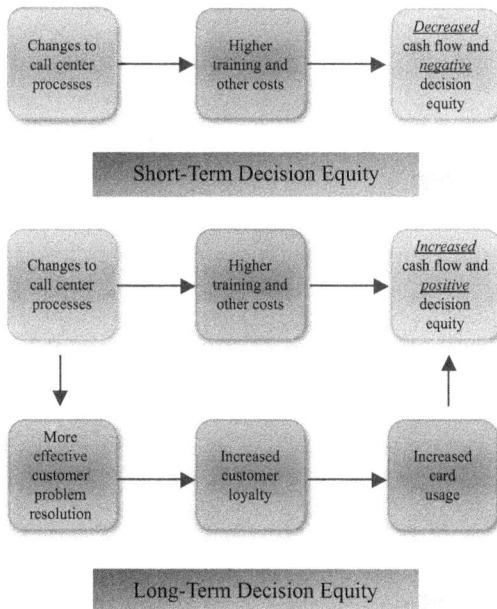

Figure 5.1. Short-term versus long-term decision equity.

term focused mostly on the higher costs associated with the process revisions in the call center, the long-term equity estimation included the benefits that accrue from improved customer loyalty.

In sharp contrast, the discovered linkages associated with the strategic option relating to a modified penalty structure for late fees were completely different. In this case, the exploration focused on the impact of late fees on subsequent customer perceptions of the credit card issuer. Specifically, the research focused on the differential impact of late fees and customer perceptions and usage of the card across *transactors* (those that pay off entire outstanding balance every month) and *revolvers* (those that do not pay off full amount every month). The net impact or the equity related to the decision of using the alternative fee structure was estimated by comparing the changes in the resulting behaviors of the two segments of customers. A similar process was repeated for all alternative decisions to discover the linkages between the action and the likely consequences. The results from each exploration were then used to assess and compare the value or equity associated with the respective decisions. Needless to say, the linkages associated with each decision were remarkably different from those for every other. Yet the alternatives could ultimately be compared on a common scale based on the decision equity associated with each.

Overall, the portfolio of analyses provided the necessary decision support to management by allowing them to objectively compare alternate strategic options under consideration using the power of data, linkages, and decision equity. Such a comparison was possible because the research project was paradigm free and spanned and linked multiple decision domains. It favored the estimation of the impact of each potential strategic decision and a computation of the decision equity through a process of data-driven verification. At the culmination of the process, all the functional managers were able to compare a diverse set of strategic options using a common language of linkages and dollars and cents. This was in sharp contrast to what we normally observe in either a paradigm-based or a silo-based culture of decision making. In this case, the call center managers did not focus exclusively on improvements in productivity within their operations or changes to the first-call resolution performance. The human resource managers did not talk about their silo-based set of metrics that tended to focus largely on employee productivity and training. Instead, the focus on *decision* equity drew linkages *across* these functional silos to unveil the impact of a diverse portfolio of decisions, each with their own unique linkages, on the strategic goals and bottom-line performance of the organization.

Defining Characteristics of Decision Equity

The aforementioned case of the credit card issuer illustrates some of the defining characteristics of decision equity. While the concept has the familiar computational underpinnings in the present value of future cash flows resulting from a decision, it has numerous distinguishing features that make it a powerful aid for making strategic marketing choices.

Paradigm Free

Perhaps the most critical difference between decision equity and other marketing measurement systems is that it is paradigm free. It is not bound either to any strategic prescription or to the sequence of consequences that follow from a strategic action. It is also not tied to the advancement of any specific metric in order to achieve a broader financial or strategic goal. Instead, it crosses functional boundaries and helps organizations draw linkages that go much beyond their silo-based paradigms. For example, depending on the context, a decision equity–based system may develop linkages spanning from innovation to human resource policies and from technology upgrades to price changes. As one can imagine, the measurement and implementation system in each case would end up focusing on a vastly different set of metrics and intermetric relationships.

How does this compare with traditional paradigm-driven approaches in marketing? Well, there are several important differences that result directly from abandoning a paradigm-based approach. For example, consider the customer satisfaction–based management paradigm. Those who follow it believe satisfaction to be the central, core metric and make it the fulcrum of critical decision making. The mental model that drives this thinking typically leads to a set of three or four initiatives. First, it almost automatically leads to the institutionalization of a customer satisfaction measurement system, typically using a series of surveys that capture changes in the level of this apparently critical metric. This tracking system is used to keep watch on satisfaction levels and judge the health of the business, at least in part, on the basis of changes in this metric. The second step involves initiatives dedicated to an understanding of the antecedents or drivers of this key metric. This involves enhancing the satisfaction measurement system and adding other variables that are believed to be the drivers of satisfaction. The third step is to identify the consequences of satisfaction to assess whether changes in the metric are resulting in the expected changes in downstream consequences, such as levels of loyalty, repeat purchase behaviors, price sensitivity, or word-of-mouth activity. And more recently, there is a move to connect changes in the level of the metric to financial consequences such as long-term profits, firm valuation, stock prices, or risk. While there is nothing fundamentally wrong in the argument that firms should strive to increase their customers' satisfaction and expect returns from customer-based investments, the paradigm may close strategic options that might be more effective than merely embracing the paradigm

Similarly, consider the brand equity–based paradigm. Once again, those who follow it treat brand equity as the central metric of interest. Much like in the satisfaction-based paradigm, investments are made in equity tracking systems followed by others to unearth its antecedents and then its downstream consequences in terms of market share gains or pricing gains. In case measures of brand equity breach preset thresholds, actions are taken to raise them again to restore the health of the brand. Once again, while brands really are valuable and watching over their health is important, if firms embrace them too closely, they are likely to close strategic pathways that may lead to long-term profitability even though they might involve bypassing the brand equity route completely.

Spans Across Multiple Silos

The second characteristic of decision equity, which stems partly from it being a paradigm-free concept, is that its span crosses functional boundaries and organizational silos. The goal of pursuing decision equity is to connect actions and decisions in any domain at one end to their ultimate consequences, which typically are in the financial or stakeholder domains, at the other. Between these two bookends, a wide variety of intermediate effects could result from the widely different possible actions.

For example, consider a nonmarketing decision such as the outsourcing of the customer service operations to an independent outside entity. In many instances, these actions are driven by strategic objectives that relate to efficiency and cost saving. Therefore, the decision itself may originate in the finance department of the organization. However, the sequence of effects that might follow the decision typically span across several functional silos. For example, on the marketing front, customer perceptions of the quality of customer service might change, which, in turn, might influence their likelihood of buying from the firm over a period. This behavioral change would influence the revenue and margin stream of the firm. On the other hand, on the human resources front, there might be cost savings accruing from a dismantling of the internal customer service operations and a reduction in the headcount and the required office space. Similarly, on the accounting front, there would be cost savings from changes in the accounting practices necessary to manage an external vendor rather than an internally staffed operation. And finally, there would be changes on the information technology front because the control systems necessary to monitor an external vendor may be significantly different from those required for an in-house operation.

This simple example illustrates a few important issues. First, even though the decision might originate in the finance area, a focus on decision equity will require coordination across several departments to realize the anticipated cost savings and revenue gains. Second, the information necessary to compute the anticipated decision equity prior to the decision as well as the actual realized equity after the decision is made again requires coordination across functional silos. Finally, the likely sequence of effects emanating from a decision will all end up being very diverse across the various functional silos.

Now if we generalize across decision domains, we can see that decision equity, because of its cross-functional underpinnings, will necessitate, maybe even force, interdepartmental coordination both at the time the decision is under consideration and later when its consequences are being evaluated. To that extent, we expect a focus on decision equity to have a very different organizational impact than more silo-centered mental models such as those that focus on customers or brands or employees. Decision equity is likely to promote the breakdown of silos and encourage a sharing of responsibilities, credit, and blame across functional boundaries, and the construction of cross-functional models of cause and effect.

Multiple Pathways and Linkages

As the previous examples show, there are many pathways from actions to profits or other terminal consequences of interest. And in an increasingly cross-functional business world, it is becoming evident that the chain of events that follow from a decision made in one domain tend to transcend functional boundaries and organizational silos. However, mental models of marketing strategy, for the most part, have not kept up with notional dissolution of intrafirm boundaries. Further, in part because they are paradigm bound, marketing practitioners do not necessarily embrace a culture of data-driven verification of linkages. Under the best-case scenario, they focus on a set of a few metrics that still operate within the confines of the functional silo. The only exception is the move to directly connect a within-silo metric with a financial outcome. An unfortunate consequence of the existing state of practice is that strategic pathways of cause and effect are constructed within functional domains and the opportunity to explore more powerful cross-functional options is foregone.

In contrast, decision equity encourages the exploration of all pathways to common ultimate goals. These pathways tend to have very different structures for the various alternatives under consideration at a point in time and also change differently across time. They also vary across firms within the same industry as well as across industrial sectors. Decision equity therefore promotes the exploration and verification of alternative linkage systems that collectively constitute a portfolio of multiple within-silo and intersilo pathways from the action to the ultimate outcome.

Focus on Actions and Terminal Metrics

Finally, a key characteristic of decision equity is a focus on the bookends, that is, on the decision at one end and the ultimate terminal metric of interest at the other. It is not tied to the promotion or optimization of intermediate metrics such as employee productivity, customer satisfaction, service quality perceptions, or price sensitivity. While in some instances, an increase in one or more of these intermediate metrics might be correlated with a rise in the terminal metric, in other instances it might not. For example, while in the case of one health care provider we observed a positive relationship between customer satisfaction and profitability, we observed the exact opposite for another. This contrast is easily accommodated within the decision equity framework because it relies on data to tell the story about the direction and strength of a link in the pathway between strategic actions and terminal outcomes.

Another key benefit of the decision equity approach is an avoidance of double counting while assessing the impact of strategic choices. If we recall the discussion in the prologue to this book, it is easy to see that some actions may have a multitude of consequences in a variety of functional domains. However, if we pursue a function-specific approach to estimating the impact of actions, it is possible that we will end up attributing the same successful outcome to multiple constituents and end up double counting the impact of the individual performance metrics. For example, as we saw, the pathway from a decision to the ultimate financial outcome might go through employees, brands, and customers. However, if we do not explore the entire pathway in one shot and do it selectively, we might be misled. We might infer that employees affect financial outcomes, as do brands and customers independently. However, in reality, they might all be the common beneficiaries of a single common action.

The decision equity framework also helps solve the metrics selection problem. As we noted in the case of the credit card issuer, in the absence of a unifying framework, constituents from each silo tend to focus on silo-specific metrics. Marketing managers, for example, may focus on changes in brand perception, call center managers might focus on the percentage of first-time resolutions, and human resource managers might focus on overall employee productivity. It is easy to see that managing these contrasting measurement systems is neither easy nor free from internal conflict. However, if the functional areas are under the common umbrella of decision equity, the silo-specific metrics have limited value and are useful only if they lie on the linkage pathway from decisions to the terminal metric. And even those that do are only valuable to the extent that they indicate the extent and direction of progress toward the ultimate financial outcome. For example, employee engagement levels are of value only for an upstream decision alternative for which the linkage pathway to the terminal metric goes through this metric.

The True Residence of Equity

One of the important management trends of the last decade is the increased emphasis on connecting nonfinancial decisions to their financial consequences. While several financial metrics can be linked to managerial actions, one that has recently gained popularity is equity. The notion of equity is borrowed from the financial principles of capitalizing future cash flows into their present value using an appropriate discounting mechanism. For example, many firms try to estimate the relationship between their investments in customer satisfaction management programs or in product development programs and their respective financial consequences. One of the metrics of interest when following these approaches is the lifetime value of each customer. And the aggregated lifetime value across the current and potential customer base is labeled customer equity. This metric represents the discounted value of the future cash flows associated with the customer base. The concepts of lifetime customer value and customer equity are then used for various strategic purposes, such as segmenting customers on the basis of high versus low value, or evaluating the relationship between customer-based rationalization programs and the value of the firm.

Now imagine a familiar situation where a firm makes a decision to let go of its unprofitable customers much like some credit card issuers and cell phone companies have recently done.[1] If the decision is correctly implemented, and if the customers that were let go were indeed unprofitable for the firm, the average lifetime value and the overall equity of the remaining customers will generally be higher than what it was before. It is also likely that the value of the firm might go up because the financial markets may reward the spinoff of unprofitable customers. Now the question is whether the increase in firm value should be attributed to the change in the customer equity of the firm. If we do a before-and-after comparison, we would indeed discover a positive correlation between the change in the firm value and the change in its customer equity. However, what really happened is that the increase in firm value and the increase in customer equity were *both* consequences of the decision to let go of unprofitable customers. Therefore, we argue that the true residence of the equity lay in the decision to rationalize the customer portfolio. The change in the value of the customer base, that is, the change in customer equity, was merely a downstream consequence of the decision. In other words, customer equity was not the cause or the source of the change in the value of the firm. Instead, it was a beneficiary of the customer portfolio rationalization *decision*. The true source of the change in firm value, that is, *the true residence of equity* was the strategic *decision* to rationalize the customer portfolio.

Similarly, the notion of brand equity is based on the premise that brands have a certain power to generate incremental cash flows for the firm over what an unbranded product in the same market might be able to. And the premise itself is true because all markets have strong and weak brands, and the financial returns associated with stronger ones tend to be higher than for weaker ones. So the natural question is whether a brand is a true residence of equity or merely a beneficiary of some strategic decisions where the equity really resides.

In order to address this issue, let us consider a few scenarios and assess the impact on a brand's equity. First, take the case of category rationalization decisions that are currently being made by many retailers.[2] For example, Wal-Mart and Kroger are increasingly reducing their portfolio of national brands and substituting them aggressively with their own private labels. Imagine that a national brand in a common category, say powdered sugar, is dropped by a retail chain across all its stores. Overnight, the entire stream of future cash flows associated with the brand's sale within the chain will now come to zero. Consequently, the equity of the brand, as we define it now, will suffer a substantial decline. However, not much fundamentally changed with the brand or what consumers thought of it. In other words, consumer preference for the brand presumably would remain the same before and after the chain's decision to pull it off the shelves. The retailer's demonstrable preference for the brand, of course, would be lower than what it was earlier. And the question we need to ask is whether the brand's equity declined. What really happened was that, given whatever strength the brand had, the retailer found it more profitable to stock the shelf with its own product. Therefore, even though the brand's strength remained the same, it's so called equity apparently declined.

Consider an alternative scenario, where a firm decided to drop the price of its core brand in order to gain or regain market share from competition. Imagine that, as a result of the decision, the brand's unit margin reduced and its overall profitability declined despite an increase in market share. Of course, depending on the size of the price cut and customers' price sensitivity, the reverse could be true as well. In either case, there would be a change in the stream of cash flows resulting from a change in the brand's price. From a computational perspective, this would reflect as a change in the equity or what is sometimes called the value of the brand. While numerically this might be true, the question again is where the residence of the equity shift really is. Is it in the brand or in the decision to alter price? To what should the change in cash flows be attributed?

More generally the question really is, what is equity and where does it really reside? Current marketing models assume or propose that it does reside in stakeholders such as employees, customers, or partners, or in entities such as brands or products. However, as the previous examples and many others later in the book illustrate, stakeholders and entities are often the *beneficiaries* of equity-enhancing or equity-damaging decisions, not the *source* of them. True equity resides in actions or strategic choices that lead to increases in cash flows or reductions in investments or both. For example, if an action is undertaken to increase the advertising spending for a specific brand, it is possible that the unit sales or price commanded by the brand might go up. However, the source of the resulting increase in equity is actually the action or decision to increase advertising. The brand is merely the beneficiary of the action and may have the increased equity attributed to it perhaps erroneously. Similarly, it is possible in this case that the increased sale came from the existing set of customers. In which case, the customer base may also be the beneficiary of the increased equity, and we may erroneously implicate it as the source.

Summary

In summary, one can think of decision equity in a number of ways. At a conceptual level, it is a philosophy or a guiding principle, which suggests that the value of decisions lies in the value of the capitalized future cash flows resulting from them. Several entities or metrics may benefit from good decisions, but the true residence of equity or its source is the decision itself. At a more concrete level, decision equity is perhaps the ultimate management metric that can be used to judge good versus bad strategic choices on the basis of their financial outcomes. The system of linkages that accompanies decision equity–based thinking can also be used as a device to cut through organizational silos and connect them through common pathways. A secondary benefit of this approach is a suppression of the importance of silo-based models and ultimately silo-based thinking. Decision equity can also be used as an evaluation system in order to devise reward structures based on true contributions to the financial outcomes of firms and prevent rewarding beneficiaries of equity enhancing decisions. Moreover, it can be used as a measure of the learning occurring within the organization. Strategic learning within this context can be thought of as acquiring the knowledge about the strength of linkages relating different actions to their consequences. And finally, the adoption of a decision equity–based framework can be used as an indicator that the organization is breaking free from paradigm-driven and silo-based thinking toward a more paradigm-free and data-driven regime.

CHAPTER 6

Understanding Decision Equity

A Flow-Based Approach

The Complexity of Strategic Marketing Decisions

As we have discussed earlier, our experience with a multitude of organizations suggests that simplified heuristics and satisficing frequently guides managers' decision-making process. This is especially true when the decisions are complex and strategic, where the range of possibilities is large, and numerous variables and outcomes often interact with each other. We find that five characteristics define this simplified decision-making process for complex, strategic choices.

1. *Organizational goals are often unclear and shift over time.* As customer preferences evolve and industries adapt, old goals become incapable of providing a sustainable path forward, and create an imperative for organizations to modify their strategic objectives. For example, the evolution of technology has completely transformed the distribution system in many industries. Songs and movies are now downloadable almost instantly from anywhere. Customers can conduct banking transactions from the comfort of their homes. Up-to-the-minute news on the Internet is posing serious challenge to traditional media vehicles, such as newspapers and magazines. Under these circumstances, a number of players in incumbent industries have had to make serious changes to their goals pertaining to a number of strategic marketing domains, including pricing, content procurement, advertising, and distribution width. Even without technological advances, other factors,

such as the entry of new competitors, variations in the health of the macroeconomy, regulation, and discrete shifts in customer preferences result in major revisions to organizational goals.

2. *Cause-and-effect chains are seldom simple and linear.* We find that when managers rely on their intuition to solve strategic problems they overwhelmingly assume simple, linear cause-and-effect relationships between upstream actions and downstream results. They tend to discount the effects of moderating factors that would attenuate or exacerbate the assumed outcomes. For example, when they contemplate a price reduction, managers automatically, and often correctly, anticipate an immediate increase in the market share of their products. However, they discount other relevant factors such as a price reduction by competitors, margin compressions in the industry, and quality signals sent by the price reduction. These and other moderating factors are almost always in play, but managers routinely ignore them and make strategic marketing decisions based on simple, linear, cause-and-effect mental models.

3. *No two decisions are likely to have the same solution.* Managers tend to minimize the stress associated with decision making, and find it easiest to dig into their own experiences when solving a problem. The application of heuristics then leads them to rely on analogies and similarities among situations to come up with old solutions to new problems. By doing so, they often minimize the search for alternate solutions, and the sufficient evaluation of these alternatives. While such a decision-making strategy is cognitively easier and less stressful, it is seldom optimal because it underplays the differences among situations while emphasizing their similarities.

4. *A rational cookie-cutter approach to decision making does not likely exist in reality.* Conflicting political interests, silo-focused local governance, precedence of personal interests over collective synergies, threatening environments, high uncertainty, and other external influences decrease the applicability of a standard cookie-cutter approach to decision making. While we tend to spend our time and energies on things within our control and the decisions we can affect, the impact of these decisions is not independent of all these external factors. Therefore, even similar decisions are articulated

differently depending on the functional expertise of the decision maker, past experience with similar problems, individual incentives, and the amount of information available. As a result, the range of solutions for two decisions that could be solved with a cookie-cutter approach turns out to be dramatically different.

5. *The speed of decision making is critical in today's environment.* More than ever before, the need to make effective decisions in short order of time is more important today than ever before. Customers have more choices and less patience, and many industries use technology effectively to get their offerings to customers at high speed. Customer dissatisfaction stories diffuse at lightning speed over the Internet and do not give management much time to respond. For example, airlines that do not engage in effective and quick service recovery after a much publicized public nightmare, such as passengers stranded on the tarmac for hours, can often face the wrath of the passengers as well as legislators. Toyota's efforts to apologize and reassure car owners in the aftermath of its quality issues was again an attempt to placate the customers before it got too late. Organizations realize that they need to gather the relevant facts at high speed and incorporate as many of them as possible in order to respond in today's fast-paced environment as quickly and as efficiently as possible. This is often a daunting task because the number of variables that can impact the observed symptom can be overwhelming, especially when an analytical and data-driven decision-making process is not in place.

Overcoming the Challenge of Complex Decisions

In this section, we discuss two approaches to make effective decisions despite the complexities associated with today's marketing problems. Our experience suggests that these recommendations can have two major positive effects. First, they foster an organizational learning environment that is fact based rather than intuition driven. Second, they help assimilate information across local silos and help everyone recognize the presence of other "moving parts" that affect the organization's ability to achieve its desired goals. Together, these two solutions—a "systems approach" and "procedural rationality"—build an organizational culture that recognizes the fluid nature of organizational goals, gives adequate consideration to possible alternatives, allows for indirect and nonlinear causal relationships, and minimizes the discounting of external factors in the decision-making process.

A Systems Approach to Marketing Decisions

A systems approach views organizations as unified entities comprising interconnected parts that "hang together" and continually affect each other across time. With a correct approach, these parts can be orchestrated to operate toward a common goal. However, if the relationship of these parts to the overall system is not fully realized, they can work at cross-purposes and hinder the achievement of the organization's goals. Therefore, effective decision making requires a universal acknowledgment of the larger system, and recognition that few marketing problems are likely to be fully located within its functional silo. More often than not, the scope of the problem and the solutions domain are likely to spread beyond the marketing silo and have broader system-wide implications.

However, each system consists of multiple local actors who have their own sets of biases and experiences. A sales manager is more in tune with the strengths of the selling arm of the organization, while a product development manager is more conversant with the research and development activities. As a result, we find that in most decision-making situations, managers tend to pay the greatest attention to the obvious local symptoms. In other words, they tend to map the strategic problem to their own domain of expertise rather than appreciate its relationship to the larger system. As a result, they ignore promising solutions that account for the systemic nature of problems even when these larger solutions hold the greatest promise.

A systems approach to decision making attempts to encourage such realization, and encourages managers to trace the potential multiplicity of causes of the problem instead of proposing a silo-based and local solution. This is analogous to how a doctor tries to identify the potential causes for a fever, a common symptom. For example, he might rule out infections and identify exhaustion as the immediate source of the fever.

Subsequently, he might diagnose hypertension as the source of exhaustion. The diagnosis would lead to medication and lifestyle changes to cure hypertension, plus advice to rest to cure exhaustion.

In our experience, we have repeatedly found evidence that a similar systems approach to decision making provides benefits that could not have been obtained in absence of such a perspective. In one such instance, a client firm was finding it difficult to capture the targeted level of market share for its digital cameras. Independent studies had shown that the quality of its product was comparable to that of others in the marketplace and their brand name was well known in the technology world even though they were relatively new to the world of digital cameras. Their prices were very competitive, and their distribution channel was able to get the product to the desired shelves in the various retail locations. However, we discovered that the problem was that each functional area—pricing, product quality, distribution, and so forth—was looking at its individual contribution in isolation but struggling to come up with an integrated solution since each of them seemed to be performing well individually.

In order to resolve the problem, we invited the multiple functional stakeholders to common meetings, and encouraged them to share their perspectives. In one such session, we asked the attendees to think of how their function contributed to the overall customer experience—before, during, and after the purchase. We repeated the instructions that the attendees should focus on the customer's experience, trading their functional hats with the customer's hat. While nothing seemed to come up at first, the solution ultimately emerged in a flash. As the group began building a blueprint of customer-centric experiences, it became obvious that the organization had provided virtually no training or education materials to the retail salespeople in order for them to advocate the product. In the absence of such efforts, the salespeople were unsure of the brand's product characteristics and shied away from recommending it to potential customers. The marketing strategy was revised, and the firm deployed substantial resources to correct the situation and has since gained market share. While, in retrospect, the solution might perhaps look straightforward, it became clear to the firm and us that the likelihood of discovering it was significantly enhanced by following a systems approach, breaking functional silos, and simultaneously deploying the resources of multiple stakeholders. Under the earlier, silo-based approach, the firm would have perhaps continued to flounder because it would have maintained its focus on product development, pricing, and branding.

Procedural Rationality

Procedural rationality is the other half of our proposed solution that leads to a search for complete and accurate information about the likely relationship between strategic choices and outcomes in order to make effective decisions. It is defined as the extent to which the decision-making process involves the collection of decision-relevant information and the analysis of this information in making the choice. The emphasis here is on "procedural" to highlight the importance of the process, and also to distinguish it from the general construct of rationality that alludes to decision maker omniscience. It therefore takes an opposing view to the "political behavior model" of decision making discussed earlier, which suggests that managers often pursue their own interests, without sharing the whole truth with one another. Such political behavior can then lead to choices based on inadequate or incorrect information, and therefore disappointing outcomes.

Fact-based decisions, on the other hand, are built upon the most comprehensive set of relevant data available, and can help improve the quality of the decision-making process. As Jeff Bezos, the chief executive officer of Amazon.com, once said,

> The great thing about fact-based decisions is that they overrule the hierarchy. The most junior person in the company can win an argument with the most senior person with regard to a fact-based decision. For intuitive decisions, on the other hand, you have to rely on experienced executives who've honed their instincts. (http://timoelliott.com/blog/2009/02/who_has_the_data.html)

In general, procedural rationality is more important in unstable environments, where things are more fluid and uncertain at any given point in time, and therefore, managers have few similar historical lessons to guide their decision-making process. On the other hand, managers in stable settings are more likely to have an experience- based understanding of their environment, and therefore a lower need to engage in information collection and analysis in order to make effective choices. However, an important deduction here is that if managers have not engaged in experience- and fact-based decision making in the past, then they will continue to make the same mistakes even in stable environments. Therefore, it is important to recognize that implementing fact-based decision making once can lead to more efficient and less erroneous decisions in the future.

The example of a retailer that we worked with illustrates a successful application of procedural rationality. In this case, the firm was seeking higher earnings from the customers that visited its retail outlets. A study designed to provide relevant information to senior executives found compelling evidence for a strong and positive link between the quality of customers' in-store experiences and their share of category purchase from the firm. In other words, the evidence suggested that customers reporting more favorable in-store experiences were more likely to spend more money in these stores. Subsequent analyses suggested that a key driver of the quality of the in-store experience was the nature of the customer interaction with the frontline retail employees. The next step in the analysis revealed that the engagement level of the frontline employees related positively to their ability to deliver superior customer experiences. Finally, there was undeniable evidence that employee empowerment had a strong impact on the level of employee engagement.

Armed with such information, the retail executives undertook a series of initiatives to better empower their employees, such that these employees could handle customer issues with greater confidence and authority. This included the development and launch of multiple initiatives, all focused on making employees more empowered within the stores. Six months later, there was compelling evidence that employees felt more empowered to handle customer issues and requests. This led to improved levels of employee engagement, delivery of superior customer experiences, and therefore more favorable customer behavior in terms of greater share allocation for the retailer. The investigation path in this case, from a strategic goal of higher earnings to a very specific action item of higher employee empowerment, emerged as the research evolved over time in its quest to finding more diagnostic and actionable information. A standard cookie-cutter approach or reliance on past experience would probably not have revealed the solution and would have led the organization down a less optimal or even an incorrect path.

Decision Flows

So far, we have proposed that we should view an organization as an interconnected system of individual parts that should be orchestrated in designing optimal solutions—a systems approach to decision making. We have also argued that it is important to incorporate a process of fact-based decision making—that is, the need for procedural rationality. Taken together, these two proposals suggest that even though the locus of an individual decision might reside within a specific organizational function or silo, there is a very good chance that both the antecedents of the problem and the consequences of the decision are likely to flow through other functions and touch points. Therefore, in order to evaluate the complete impact of an individual decision, facts and data would need to *flow* both into and out of the decision across the immediate boundaries of the local function.

For example, a decision to provide additional product training to the representatives of a pharmaceutical firm could lead to better physician experiences during the call by the representative, which, in turn, might then translate to a higher number of scripts written by these physicians for the drug in focus. Now in order to assess the equity residing in the decision to provide additional product training, the training manager can incorporate the data from the anticipated downstream flow of events including the number of additional calls, changes in physicians' evaluation of the focal drug, the number of additional scripts generated, and their financial consequence. Rust and his colleagues discuss a similar example of a hotel in their work on the "Return on Quality." In this instance, they evaluated the impact of increased time spent by the housekeeping staff in cleaning the guest rooms. They showed that the increased time spent on cleaning resulted in improved guest perceptions of the cleanliness of their rooms and bathrooms. Consequently, guests had a more favorable overall perception of their room and the stay, which resulted in higher loyalty toward the hotel brand. This flow of effects was used to evaluate the financial return on the quality initiative, which was to increase the average time spent for cleaning each room. What is important to note here is that even seemingly tactical decisions require a fact-based study of the flow of effects across multiple time periods and touchpoints for an estimation of their total impact. For every such evaluation, it is important to identify and operationalize the flow of upstream and downstream effects surrounding the decision, the time lag associated with these effects, and their possible interaction with other organizational decisions.

In recognizing the systems approach to decision making, quality and six sigma experts separate the various relationships of an individual organizational part to other parts as being an upstream or a downstream relationship. Let us stay with the same example of "cleaner hotel rooms" as a focal node in a decision flow. The upstream flow in this case would start from the management's decision to increase the time spent per room by the housekeeping staff. The next node would be the actual time spent by the staff, followed by the average levels of the cleanliness of the rooms themselves, the focal node. It is important not only to recognize the presence of such flow relationships but also to calibrate them by estimating their direction and magnitude. For example, every additional minute spent per room might not provide equivalent incremental improvement in cleanliness. Similarly, customer perceptions of room cleanliness might taper off after a certain incremental time investment. Most importantly, other actions, such as different cleaning supplies, or higher levels of automation, might be able to achieve the same outcome: a clean room. However, despite a common intermediate metric, a cleaner room, the overall decision flows following from these alternative choices may look vastly different.

Downstream flow relationships, on the other hand, are the consequential outcomes in terms of the benefit and losses that result from the changes in the focal node and the associated metric. In the case of room cleanliness as the focal node, a higher level of performance could potentially lead to more favorable customer evaluations of their specific room, the overall property, or the hotel brand itself. This could translate into a greater propensity to choose the brand, pay a higher price per room-night, or utilize more paid utilities and services on site. More importantly, there would be parallel flows on the employee side. Depending on the upstream decision, employee effort could go either up or down, which could have a favorable or unfavorable effect on their satisfaction, and on their decision to stay or leave. In turn, this chain of events may increase or decrease the cost of retaining, hiring, and training employees. Other potential flows on the cost side of each action would account for changes in the cost of supplies and employee time.

Firms need to evaluate both upstream and downstream relationships not only in terms of their mere presence but also in terms of their direction, shape, and magnitude. It is critically important for them to determine these flows in order to evaluate whether the investment associated with the primary upstream decision will or will not have any equity. If there is no equity, then management may consider investing elsewhere to optimize its resource allocation. For example, it might want to conduct similar flow analyses for other potential choices, such as replacing existing beds with more comfortable ones, redesigning the lobby, upgrading the television sets in rooms, or providing free Internet service. A comparison of flows across the decisions would reveal which decisions have greater or less equity as compared to the others.

Variation in Strategic Flows

It is also important to realize that the structure of flows varies significantly across contexts. For example, the flows from the same decision, say increasing room cleanliness, tends to vary significantly across market segments. Consequently, the equity associated with improving room cleanliness is very different for a luxury hotel chain as compared to a chain in the economy segment. For the luxury brand, clean rooms are likely to be viewed as a basic table-stakes requirement, while for an economy chain, cleanliness can be a performance driver and significantly influence the favorability of customer experiences. The luxury chain on the other hand would not have survived the competitive landscape if it did not already have very clean rooms. The flows are also very different within the same product segment but across two chains with different baseline levels of cleanliness. They are also different across customer segments. We have observed that service quality is typically more important for business customers, brand appeal is relatively more desirable for conspicuous consumption categories, and price tends to be a critical driver of customer retention for commodity goods and services. Finally, the downstream flows from two reasonably comparable decisions, say increasing room cleanliness versus upgrading the television set in rooms, may potentially have widely different flow patterns.

The second important characteristic of flows is that the time lag between certain upstream and downstream relationships can vary. Let us take a personal example to illustrate the point. Imagine that you just moved to a new city to take up a new job, and as you settled into your house, you made three common household purchases. On the very first evening, you went to the neighborhood grocery store to buy things for dinner. As soon as you walked in, imagine that you were pleasantly surprised by the clean and well-lit stores, the competitive prices, and the friendly checkout clerk who offered to assist you with loading the groceries in your car on a snowy evening. The next morning, you woke up to realize you needed coffee and bread and went back to the store immediately—there was almost no lag between your attitudes and behavior toward the store. In this same trip the next morning, you also stopped by the bank in the store and got information on opening a checking account for payroll and other daily transactions. Satisfied with the offer of the bank, and driven by its proximity to your new home, you opened a checking account, and for the next few weeks, you had no unpleasant experiences with the bank. A few weeks later, when the need arose to open a savings account, you went back to the same bank. In this case, the bank accrued the benefit of providing a good customer experience after a period of time. Finally, as you were settling in, you decided that you needed to buy a new desktop computer for your new home. You went through a careful process and then bought a good deal online directly from the manufacturer. As you have been working with the machine over the last few weeks, you have been happy with the performance, and you cannot believe that you got it at such a bargain price. However, it might easily be a couple of years, if not more, before you will have the need to buy another computer for your household.

Similarly, you can think of all recent organizational decisions you have made, and estimate the time over which the flow of effects might manifest itself. In a marketing context, three of the four classic Ps of the marketing mix—product, place, and promotion—are sticky and have long lag periods associated with decisions. A product perceived to be of poor quality cannot make overnight claims of superior quality. Think of American versus Japanese cars before the Toyota braking problems. Customer quality evaluations can be very sticky and customers can be unforgiving, even if the American manufacturers provide objectively better quality. Likewise, the benefits of improved distribution (place) and promotion might not have instantaneous reactions from the marketplace. Of these four classic Ps of the marketing mix, price is the least sticky. Changes in price get an immediate reaction from the marketplace but it also does not last for a very long time.

Finally, our examples so far have been very isolated in that we have assumed that an organization implements only one decision at a given point in time and that future decisions are in abeyance until this decision has flown through all its upstream and downstream relationships. In reality, several organizational decisions are implemented simultaneously or within short spans of time, and it becomes important to understand the interactions among them. For example, the decision to spend extra minutes to clean a hotel room may be made in conjunction with the decision to buy cheaper and inferior brands of cleaning supplies. As a result of such a composite decision, customers might see no improvement or even deterioration in the cleanliness of the room. Similarly, if the extra housekeeping budget comes at the expense of much-needed investments in more comfortable beds—cleaner rooms might not always lead to more favorable overall perceptions of the hotel property. How many of us would want a clean bathroom but an uncomfortable bed to spend the night? Therefore, flows need to be evaluated based on whether the action being contemplated is a singular or a composite decision.

Here is another case study to illustrate the point. A banking firm faced a decision to reduce the number of tellers in its branches in order to save costs and encourage more customers to use other modes of banking such as the automated teller machines (ATMs) and web-based banking. The staff reduction was seen as providing immediate reduction in labor costs for the organization, making it a tempting decision to implement. A systems- and fact-based approach to decision making, however, encouraged management to evaluate the overall downstream impact of staff reduction on higher wait times for in-branch customers, which in turn might have led to customer exodus. In other words, even though there was a single decision on the table there were two countervailing flows to consider. On the one hand, there was the flow associated with reduced cost. On the other hand, there was a parallel flow associated with higher customer exodus. Further, the time frames for the flow effects to be observed were very different. The impact of the cost reduction would be visible instantly, whereas the potential customer exodus would unfold over a longer period. While we repeatedly see this problem, in this case the data suggested that a selective staff reduction strategy was prudent. It was determined that the reductions would initially take place in neighborhoods with a younger and well-educated customer base that had already begun migrating to alternative channels that the bank was interested in maintaining. Similarly, in the case of a credit card operator that was interested in assessing its program of giving cash back to its customers for purchase activity, the data suggested that the incremental customer loyalty associated with this cash back was greater than the hit to the bottom line, suggesting that the bank should continue with the practice.

Strategic Flowprinting

A flowprint is the chart of the upstream and downstream relationships associated with a decision. Let us take a common example of an organization that plans to boost customer satisfaction with the firm. After all, being more customer centric seems like the correct thing to do in most competitive marketplaces. A flowprint would require asking some key questions to relevant, cross-functional stakeholders, and then drawing a system of relationships such as the one shown here for a business-to-business (B2B) technology supplier (Figure 6.1). On the downstream side, for example, the flowprint process might help better understand the financial justification for customer centricity—more satisfied customers might buy other product lines from the technology supplier, buy more units of various products, be willing to pay higher prices, and be more willing to recommend the product to others and therefore generating incremental revenue for the firm. The assumed financial returns of customer centricity are laid out and detailed through a flowprinting process. Similarly, the upstream relationships might be used to identify levers

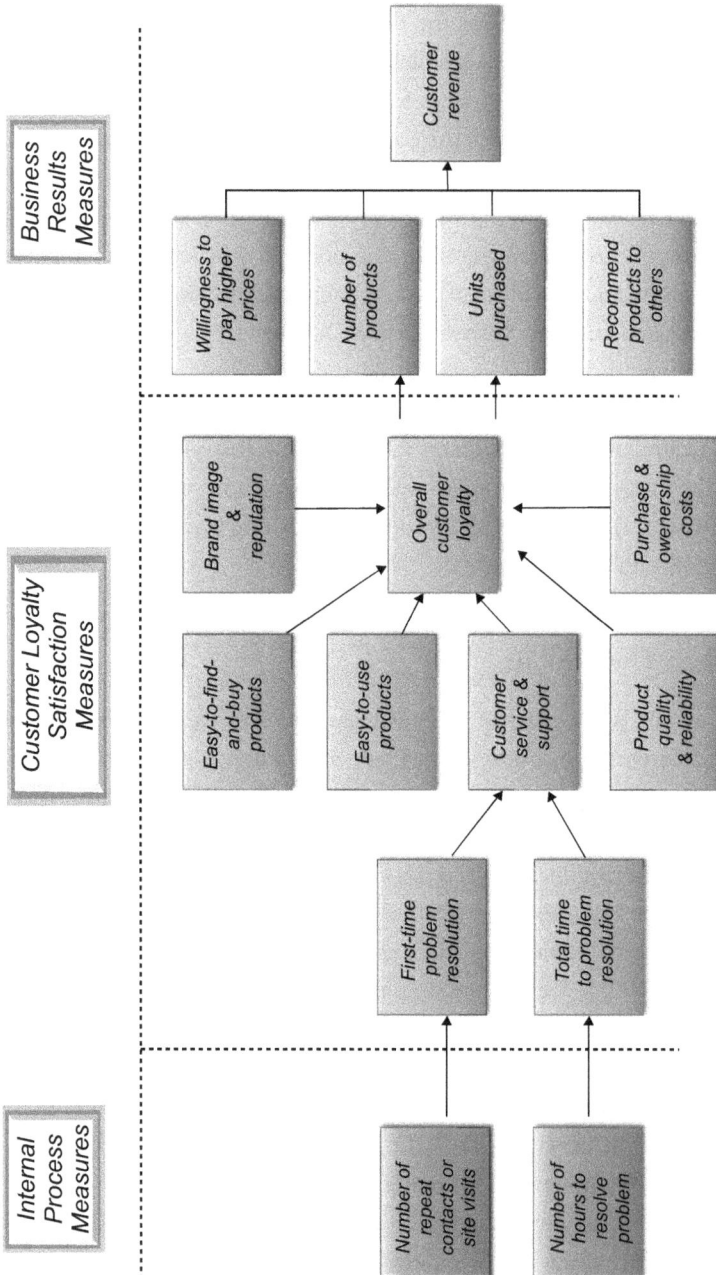

Figure 6.1. Flowprint: An example.

to pull making the organization more customer centric. These might include, for example, investments in brand equity, product quality, and so forth. The flowprint depicted in this illustrative example is a simplified version of more detailed flowprints that are used in actual implementation of strategic decisions.

The flowprint approach is not a cookie-cutter approach to decision making, and has some important characteristics. It encourages the need for systems-based thinking where individual silos are seen as interconnected components of the overall organizational system. It fosters a fact-based decision-making culture wherein managerial knowledge is used to develop hypothesized relationships that are then tested and validated using the available data. Because the process involves relevant stakeholders in hypothesis articulation, flowprinting earns stakeholder engagement by using their inputs into the formulation of linkages for further exploration. Stakeholder engagement also comes from the fact that flowprinting does not impose a standard model across geographies and industries. It is a customized effort that examines the set of relationships articulated by the decision makers themselves. The flowprinting starts a process of ownership because the proposed set of relationships are hypothesized by the individuals who themselves are stakeholders in the outcome of the process. Finally, flowprinting establishes cross-functional participation because it is rooted in the interconnected components of the organization.

Linking Key Metrics Through Flowprinting

A key advantage of the flowprint is its ability to draw relationships among key metrics that are used regularly in various organizations to gauge the health of the firm. Some might even argue that managers spend an inordinate amount of their time monitoring and influencing these key metrics to enhance organizational performance. Some very commonly used metrics include measures of defect and rework, problem incidence and resolution, product availability, measures of product and service quality, customer satisfaction, brand equity, market share, growth, revenue, margins, and profitability. This list is by no means exhaustive, but we have observed that across industries these metrics are often reviewed with zest and interest, as though they were gauges indicating if the organization is headed in the right direction. More often than not, these metrics are viewed as isolated numbers and not viewed in the context of a systems approach to organizational management.

In a recent client engagement, for instance, we observed two teams that worked on improving brand equity and customer satisfaction scores in the marketplace. Ironically, these teams worked in independent silos and never had an opportunity to cross-pollinate their thinking and efforts. Their measurement approaches were thus very different and divergent. The result was a discordance of scores, where the organization continued to see improvements in brand equity scores, with an erosion of customer satisfaction scores. The teams however never got the opportunity, or for that matter expressed an interest, in getting together to ask the question about how could they have a stronger brand if the customers are increasingly unhappy with their experiences. After all, customer satisfaction is a key pillar of a strong brand! Likewise, in many organizations that we have consulted with, we found high walls separating employee and customer measurements. One part of the organization could thus make claims about improvements in the engagement of its workforce, including customer-facing employees, without ever examining if such improvements led to superior customer experiences. For one service organization, we found that not only was such a relationship missing but also no attempts had been made to seek association between measures of employee engagement and employee productivity or reduction in voluntary employee turnover.

Thus while key organizational metrics then capture important performance information, a flowprinting approach to decision making brings value by identifying the relationship among these metrics. It helps draw systematic conclusions among the observed phenomenon instead of just observing the more noticeable symptoms. If you can think of a series of gauges connected to each other in a series of consciously designed patterns, then a flowprinting approach does not just study the change in reading of an individual gauge and then recommend a solution or cause. Instead, it identifies the relationship among the observed movement in other gauges to identify possible causes and propose correction, if required. Such investigation is conducted until the management can identify directly actionable causes that can be altered to make downstream changes.

In one such implementation, we observed that a retail institution was unable to retain a majority of its customers. Such churn was proving to be very expensive for the organization, and therefore it undertook an evaluation of probable causes. A flowprint session was conducted at the onset of the investigation, and over the next few weeks, the research led us down a path wherein we observed that in the recent past these customers had reported less favorable perceptions of their shopping experience at the store outlets. Within the same time period, we also observed eroding levels of engagement among employees, including the frontline employees that worked at these stores and interacted with the customers. When we investigated further, we discovered that because of certain changes in corporate policies in the recent past, employees perceived a reduction in their benefits received, while other organizations were actually providing similar or improved benefits to their employees. The employees were clearly unhappy with the change, especially as those were more plentiful economic times, and this also led to an exodus of the more experienced and higher performing employees to other competitive retail organizations. The retention of less-engaged employees and the departure of better performers therefore led to inferior customer shopping experiences.

When management discussed the issue internally, they realized that one of their internal communication issues seemed to have misfired. Management had actually not reduced the quality of benefits it provided to its employees, and had only enhanced the flexibility to move these benefits to suit individual situations. For instance, an employee and spouse could cash in on the health care benefits of one of them since they both could be covered by the policy of the other partner. The communication around the increased flexibility however was not perceived as such by the employees, who misconstrued management action as one of financial stringency. Armed with this information, management launched an intense campaign to correct employee perceptions, launched a web-based campaign solely for this purpose, and held information sessions to provide accurate information around the changes. We then went back after a period of 6 months and observed that the investment seemed to have worked in the expected direction. Employee engagement levels had risen, customers were reporting more favorable in-store experiences, and customer churn was on the decline. Thus the movement of the customer retention gauge was systematically identified to a cause that could be directly acted upon.

Developing Strategic Flowprints

A typical flowprint is developed in an interactive, half-day work session with a team of cross-functional stakeholders, and is customized to each business unit, and sometimes to individual customer segments within a business unit. The output of such a session is a business model that draws out possible upstream and downstream relationships associated with the business objectives under consideration. These relationships are drawn out from a customer-centric perspective, that is, how do the upstream activities impact customer experience, and how do changes to such experience lead to changes in downstream measures? Beyond the benefits discussed here for undertaking a flowprinting approach to decision making, there is also published evidence to support its need. A *Harvard Business Review* study published a few years ago[1] presented evidence that while many companies regularly collect data on various performance measures, few attempt to draw relationships across these silo-based measures. The study concluded however that more successful companies have achieved superior performance by choosing their performance measures based on causal models, which layout possible cause-and-effect relationships that may exist between the chosen drivers of strategic success and outcomes. The study found that organizations implementing such an approach were able to achieve 3% higher return on assets (ROA) and 5% higher return on equity (ROE) vis-à-vis companies that did not deploy such a framework.

Attendees of the half-day flowprinting workshop walk out with a heightened appreciation of how the various performance metrics they monitor and try to affect on an ongoing basis are really linked to each other in a net of relationships. While some of these relationships might be obvious, it still helps to validate their presence and strength. Being customer centric, for instance, seems such an obvious relationship—more satisfied customers should engage in behaviors that should make the firm financially successful. However, the flowprint participation often leads the audience to ponder over some tough questions, such as whether the relationship would hold true for all customers. One such observation, for instance, led us to observe that only 30% of a firm's customers were profitable, while it actually lost money on the remaining 70% of customers. The question that arises is whether, in this case, the firm should work on maximizing customer satisfaction to reap benefits across the board, or should it focus only on the profit generating customers? In other flowprint sessions, the audience has often pondered if they have been buying customer loyalty by spending excessively to please customers. What if these customers report more favorable attitudes as an outcome of the firm efforts but do not provide adequate returns to recoup such efforts? Can this then mean that the firm could be congratulating itself for improvements in customer satisfaction scores, even though there might not always be a reason to rejoice?

In one flowprinting session for a utility firm, for example, we were informed that the call centers treated high- and low-value customers identically. This firm does business in a nonmonopoly footprint, and customers have a choice of switching their utility supplier. To generalize, the firm had two types of customers—one set that had been with the firm for many years and paid a sizeable bill every month, while the other was a group of customers that switched suppliers every few months and was persistently delinquent in paying their utility bills. The firm initiated and implemented a uniform policy around late or missed payment for each of these two groups of customers, without recognizing that for one set of these customers it was habitual behavior, while for the other a missed payment often related to an outlier incident such as a long vacation during which the payment date fell. When we looked at data for each of these two customer groups, we observed that, unhappy with being treated harshly for missing an isolated payment, the high worth and long tenure customers began switching to competition, which was happy to have them. Since these households were no longer customers, they did not receive the customer satisfaction survey, and the pool of survey respondents shifted to the lower tenure customer group, which was happy with the aggressive price they received in switching to this firm during their short stint with the firm, before they were forced out because of their payment behavior. Survey-based customer satisfaction scores thus started improving, and it took an overall systems approach, wherein these scores were linked to decreases in average household level revenue, to recognize the complete picture. The utility firm immediately took corrective action and started adopting more forgiving policies for the long-tenure and high-value customers. When customers contacted the call centers, their phone numbers were used to route customers through preferred versus general queues, and the representatives were empowered to make decisions based on a customer grading system—higher value customers were given more flexibility and leniency in paying their bill. Lack of a systems approach would have let the bleeding go on for much longer, much like a previous case study, where reduction in the number of tellers boosted short-term profits but led down a steep slope of customer exodus.

Measurement Myopia

The overall purpose of this chapter is to correct what we believe is "measurement myopia." As organizational decision makers, we all get so entrenched in our functional responsibilities that we often fail to see the forest from the trees. Through the case studies discussed here, it should be obvious that we all are quick to laud our efforts without pausing and confirming our hypotheses. Marketing managers feel happy when customer satisfaction scores improve. The fact that these could come from generally benevolent times, departure of the most profitable customers, or other causes does not seem to faze them. Some such managers might also relentlessly pursue perfection in customer satisfaction scores, without estimating the return on such investments. Similarly, human resource managers might be relieved about improvements in employee engagement scores, without validating if such improvements are showing the desired benefits of higher employee productivity and tenure, or superior customer experiences. No—we all feel that such evidence is not necessary, and in fact, if the search for such evidence leads to a contrary observation, then the joy might be short-lived.

CHAPTER 7

Linkage Analysis

The Engine That Powers Decision Equity

Introducing Linkage Analysis

The core concept of "linkage analysis" is to connect information and feedback from various sources in order to support the decision-making processes at the firm. As we will discuss through case studies in this chapter, these sources could include survey and nonsurvey customer data, operational data, and financial metrics. They can potentially span the organizational workforce, current and potential customers, and other internal and external stakeholders. For example, the process at a large retailing organization started by exploring the linkages between survey-based overall customer attitudes and store-level financial performance. The initial objective of the linkage exercise was to test and validate the hypothesis that stores with more favorable customer attitudes generate higher store profits. However, as the process unfolded, the research objective expanded to include three other sources of relevant data—associate engagement for the store employees, relevant process data such as the productivity of each store, and store neighborhood demographic data, including median age and household income. A more comprehensive linkage analysis, in this case, was then able to bring together these diverse but relevant sources of data to provide valuable information to the management.

Results of the linkage analysis confirmed that stores with higher levels of employee engagement were more capable of generating greater customer loyalty. Loyalty in turn led to more favorable customer behavior in these stores, characterized by larger basket size in terms of dollar value as well as the number of units in the basket. Further, the analysis confirmed that the rewards of customer loyalty were almost instantaneous, and there was very little, if any, lag between positive customer attitudes and favorable customer behavior.

Other sources of data provided additional valuable information. For instance, we were able to identify two important drivers of customer loyalty—"store productivity" and the "age of the store." This organization had been focusing on higher productivity in its outlets to generate greater profits. However, the analysis revealed that productivity levels above a certain threshold level adversely affected long-term store profitability. The negative relationship was associated with more unfavorable customer experiences in the highly productive stores where customers felt rushed and disliked the absence of adequate floor staff to assist them. This led to a decline in customer perceptions of their service experiences at the stores and their migration to competitors. The linkage approach was thus able to deploy multiple sources of data to explicate the negative effects of productivity gains on financial performance and discover the mediating role of customer perceptions. The age of the store was also found to influence the quality of service experience. Stores that were older than a certain threshold age had a dramatic drop in customer perceptions. Customers felt that these stores were run down, the aisles were too narrow, and the parking facilities were unsafe after dark. Finally, linkage analysis was able to identify neighborhood demographics that had the strongest impact on store-level profitability. Specifically, the median household size and household income in the neighborhoods around a property had a strong impact on store profitability. Two retail stores with identical levels of employee engagement and customer loyalty could therefore have substantial differences in profit because of their locations.

From the perspective of senior management, the value of the linkage analyses came from being able to bring together sources of data that had until then resided in independent locations within the organization. The ability to link these data in a set of comprehensive models allowed them to recognize and appreciate the linkages among the various performance metrics, their antecedents, and other uncontrollable factors. As a result of these analyses, management was able to allocate its resources more judiciously by comparing the impact of investments say in building and infrastructure improvements with say investing in associate engagement initiatives, because all these decisions had been linked to the same end result—the bottom-line financial performance of the organization.

Defined formally then, "linkage analysis" is the process of connecting multiple sources of organizational data to provide enhanced decision support that can improve the overall performance of the organization. The strategic and research objectives of the organization, as well as availability of relevant information needed to perform the analyses, drive the selection of the data sources. While the aforementioned retailing case study used multiple sources of data, a typical linkage project usually starts with fewer data sources. For example, a typical linkage analysis within the customer care environment might involve bringing together associate engagement and customer experience data to examine and demonstrate that more engaged employees are able to provide better customer experiences during call center transactions. Over time however, these analyses typically broaden their scope to include data on other relevant metrics of customer experience such as wait time, hold time, talk time, and after-call wrap time to understand the impact of these measures on the quality of customer experience.

The Academic Foundations of Linkage Analysis

As discussed earlier, finding data to analyze is less of a challenge for decision makers in the current environment of data explosion. In order to improve their ability to make superior decisions, managers today are showing an increased interest in models that can help them methodically sieve through the wealth of information currently at their disposal. This newfound interest has led to a review of various new and existing management frameworks, but for the purpose of our discussion, we focus on four of the more popular candidates: the "balanced scorecard," the "service profit chain," the "Malcolm Baldrige National Quality Awards criteria," and the "action profit linkage model." While each of these four frameworks has clearly provided a unique contribution to the development of management thinking, at their core they all provide the reader with a systematic process of identifying, measuring, and monitoring performance metrics that are most important for the success of the firm. To varying extent, each framework encourages decision makers to broaden their perspective beyond individual organization silos and understand the possible linkages among seemingly disparate measures such as employee engagement, customer loyalty, operational efficiency, and financial performance.

The balanced scorecard[1] enables stakeholders to manage their organization more effectively, by providing a framework that allows them to systematically identify important performance metrics across key functions of the organization. These functions include the internal processes of the organization including the performance of its workforce, the attitudes and behaviors of its customers in the marketplace, and key financial measures such as revenue and profit accrued over a period. The key thesis of this holistic and organization-wide perspective is to caution decision makers against a myopic focus on a single set of performance measures, such as short-term financial metrics. For instance, a credit card issuer focused on short-term profitability might undertake an initiative to increase the "late fees" it charges its customers. This might, however, lead to greater customer resentment with the card and lower usage. The intent to boost profits in the short term might then actually lead to eroded customer loyalty, increased customer exodus, and therefore a long-term decline in the financial performance of the issuer. In such a situation, the balanced scorecard framework can provide an early warning signal by reporting ongoing erosions in customer loyalty tied to the late fees.

The key objective of the service profit chain[2] is to demonstrate that higher levels of service employee engagement lead to enhanced customer loyalty, which in turn leads to greater financial success. The framework was instrumental in reinforcing the importance of the relationships among internal measures such as employee engagement, external measures such as customer loyalty, and the financial success of the service organizations. We frequently witness such enterprise-wide relationships in many industries wherein, for instance, management commitment to provide tools and resources to its workforce leads to improvements in its level of engagement. Improved engagement, especially among the customer-facing employees of the firm, then leads to improvements in customer loyalty. Higher loyalty, in turn, generates sales growth through more favorable customer purchasing behavior. For example, in the case of a logistics organization, we observed that customers who reported favorable interactions with the sales team and the pickup and delivery employees were more likely to allocate a greater share of their shipping needs to the firm, which in turn led to greater revenue and profit.

The Malcolm Baldrige National Quality Awards criteria[3] were instituted to recognize domestic firms that could serve as a role model for others, and increase the competitiveness of the U.S. economy in the global marketplace. These criteria allow an organization to monitor its progress along a set of very detailed and exhaustive performance measures. These measures cover the expanse of organizational functioning, including the performance of the leadership, employee engagement, efficiency and efficacy of internal processes, the feedback from customers, and the financial performance of the firm. The framework emphasizes not only the results achieved on these performance measures but also the approach and deployment of various initiatives that can help the organization sustain such results. In one case study in the technology sector for instance, we witnessed that management's commitment to improving the efficiency of its internal operations in the customer support centers led to reduction in problem resolution time, which in turn improved the feedback the organization received from its customers in the marketplace. Over time, such improvements in customer experiences led to higher customer loyalty for the firm and more favorable trends in the financial performance of the organization. The firm was able to draw such meaningful linkages because it had measured its performance on different performance metrics such as employee engagement, problem resolution time, customer feedback, and financial activity generated from these customers. More importantly, these measures were stored in databases that could be connected to each other for deriving meaningful linkages among the variables. The key benefit was that improvement targets such as employee engagement and problem resolution success are since regularly quantified in terms of a common language—their financial impact. Previously, the bottom-line impact of such targets was never estimated making the targets themselves less meaningful to top management.

The action profit linkage model[4] maps out a structured relationship among the various internal and external success factors of an organization. Unlike other linkage models, it proposes a *flexible*, discovery-based approach to understanding the true linkages between the portfolio of actions performed by the firm and the financial metrics like long-term profitability or value. It covers all organizational domains and functions and recommends that data and statistical evidence rather than structured prior beliefs drive the linkage analysis. It is not forward prescriptive and does not advocate a suggested course of action for all organizations or for all problem domains. Instead, it suggests that linkages connecting cause and effect could vary significantly across actions and across firms. By implication, it suggests that firms should consider building linkage models backward from the final effect to most appropriate actions in order to discover the best causal pathways. In contrast to the three other models discussed previously, the action profit linkage model encourages a paradigm-free approach to linkage analysis and advocates a sharp focus on *actions* and their *ultimate consequences* rather than on any intermediate metric pertaining to employees, customers, efficiency, or costs. It urges organizations to build a repository of linkages through repeated applications of linkage analysis in order to learn the structure of the causal pathways from specific actions to their desired terminal outcomes.

While each of these aforementioned models has provided valuable and unique contribution to the overall development of the management literature, at their core they all have at least five common elements (Figure 7.1). Together, these elements provide a compelling case for linking key metrics that typically reside across various organizational silos that must be collectively viewed as parts of a dynamic and interconnected system.

1. *The need for holistic and enterprise-wide performance measurement.* All the management frameworks discussed here emphasize the need for a holistic and systems-based approach to enterprise-wide performance measurement. Despite this call, we often find that firms, both Fortune 500 companies as well as smaller organizations, fail to take a global view to decision making. Instead, functional silos within the organization, such as human resources or marketing, continue to focus on feedback they gather from their own key stakeholders, without reviewing how such measurement fits into the overall functioning of the firm. Such myopia can be traced to the legacy and history of various organizational silos, the support for certain mental models and metrics among the C-level executives of the firm, as well as uncertainty about the designated executive responsible for a cross-functional view of the organization.

2. *The need for multidimensional performance measurement and evaluation.* Organizational measurement should include valid and reliable[5] measures of financial as well as nonfinancial metrics. The frameworks suggest that a common linkage system should bind several measures, such as economic profit and employee engagement, productivity and customer loyalty. They also advocate multiperiod measures, such as leading and lagging indicators, in order to trace the impact of current levels of one measure, such as customer loyalty, on the future levels of other downstream measures, such as financial performance. However, we regularly witness that in the absence of a linkage-driven mind-set, firms allocate their measurement dollars disproportionately to one silo, resulting in a poor measurement architecture that is short on information on areas of performance critical to organizational success. For instance, it is not uncommon to find firms that support multiple, and often redundant, customer loyalty studies but have no measurement system in place to gauge the level of workforce engagement.

3. *The need to link, integrate, and align performance measures.* The academic frameworks discussed earlier all advocate the need for key organizational measures to link and align toward providing compelling evidence of organizational performance. For instance, organizations should confirm that improvements in attitudinal measures of customer loyalty, such as ratings of overall satisfaction, are positively associated with and measures of financial success such as share of wallet, revenue, margin, and profit derived from these customers. Similarly, organizations should invest in confirming other key linkages, such as those between measures of internal operational efficiency, or the ability to resolve the problem quicker, and customer feedback on the quality of the transaction.

4. *The need to use these measures to drive enterprise alignment, transformation, and growth.* The ability to take a holistic view to organizational decision making, as advocated by various academic frameworks, allows managers to compare alternate resource allocation decisions on common metrics of financial outcomes. This provides valuable decision support to senior management in identifying key initiatives necessary to ensure a sustained and healthy growth of their firm. For

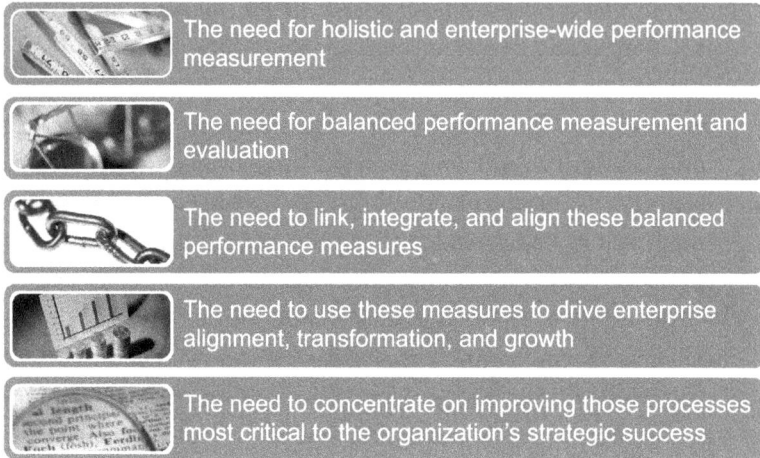

The need for holistic and enterprise-wide performance measurement

The need for balanced performance measurement and evaluation

The need to link, integrate, and align these balanced performance measures

The need to use these measures to drive enterprise alignment, transformation, and growth

The need to concentrate on improving those processes most critical to the organization's strategic success

Figure 7.1. The common elements.

example, understanding the relative impact of technology improvements versus employee performance in a customer support environment can allow management to allocate resources more effectively toward delivering customer-centric experiences that would justify such investments through enhanced customer loyalty and its downstream financial consequences.

5. *The need to concentrate on improving critical processes.* Overall, the policy advocated by the preceding academic frameworks toward a holistic, enterprise-wide, and integrated measurement system can eventually allow managers to contribute to organizational success by concentrating on those action items that are most critical for success. Organizations that follow this approach can better generate and measure their "return on actions" by identifying the bottom-line impact of undertaking various initiatives. In addition, the cross-functional requirements for such a measurement system can help remove inefficiencies resulting from a silo-based data collection and action planning approach that emphasizes the optimization of function level metrics rather than overall organizational success.

The Benefits of Linkage Analysis

Linkage analysis is the next step from intuition-based or inflexible mental model–based decision making. It takes an organization beyond just using metrics in the form of dashboards or scorecards to understanding the complex relationships among the drivers of business success. In our view, linkage analyses provide an antidote to the problems that are associated with simple, intuition-based mental models. As we noted earlier, organizations are becoming increasingly complex, more geographically distributed, and often dependent on a consortium of loosely linked entities that jointly produce the outputs of interest. In such complex environments, simple decision rules such as mental models, fundamental intuition, scorecards, or rules of thumb may be insufficient or suboptimal in driving strategic choices and business outcomes. In most cases, managers have to deal with several moving parts, and it might not be feasible or easy to comprehend how they move and work together. Therefore, managers might ignore parts of the problem that are difficult to comprehend or for which reliable data might be missing. Alternatively, they might verify some of these relationships on a one-time, ad hoc basis and rely on them over time and across problem classes.

Linkage analysis provides a rational and fact-based alternative to these suboptimal options and allows organizations to draw meaningful relationships among the various moving parts of an organizational system. For example, it allows firms to see if actions designed to boost customer loyalty indeed raise revenues and lower customer acquisition costs. It also allows them to observe whether the nature and size of these relationships is stable or changing over time. Overall, while there are several major advantages of using linkage analysis to support strategic decision making, we believe that some of the critical ones are described here.

Promoting a Culture of Verification-Based Management

One of the indirect but extremely important benefits of linkage analysis is that it builds and promotes a culture of verification-based management. Employees at all levels in the organization understand that decision making is driven by data and verifiable relationships that can be tracked over a period. Over time, the use of a broad swath of data to drive the organization becomes an integral part of it and is implicitly absorbed into its culture. This suppresses gut-feel or beliefs-based choices and tends to drive the organization toward superior decision making and closer to optimal choices.

Formalizing Learning

Organizations that adopt linkage analysis as an integral part of how they make strategic choices tend not to think of these analyses as a one-time, isolated event. Over time, these analyses tend to increase in scope and uncover linkages that were until then not understood and discovered. Second, tracking systems become part of a culture of verification-based management and *key linkages* rather than key metrics are watched using repeated measures. Both a repeated application of linkage models and the increase in the scope of these models over time provide information through linkages that the organization can learn from. Managers and executives are able to learn about critical linkages that drive firm performance, the best measures for each metrics involved in the linkages, and the evolution of the web of linkages over time.

Working With Causal Webs

In common parlance, when we say cause and effect, we seem to give an impression that the two are directly and closely connected. However, for most higher order strategic problems, the connections are neither direct nor extremely close. Therefore, managers and executives need to be able to conceptualize these causal relationships in terms of a web of interconnected variables that may demonstrate a complex set of mutual dependencies. We find that without the aid of an appropriate set of tools, and the learning that comes from their repeated application, it is difficult for managers to think, plan, and strategize in terms of webs. Outputs from linkage analyses, especially when presented in visual and graphic form, tend to promote strategic thinking in terms of a web of relationships, not merely direct cause and effect. Therefore, managers working with linkage analyses are able to concurrently account for a larger number of factors, issues, and stakeholders in their decision-making process.

Testing and Rebuilding Mental Models

In our experience, we find that most organizations invest little in verifying the mental models that they assume drive the dynamics of their business. And even in the rare case where this happens, it is done in a piecemeal rather than a systematic way. In either case, organizations end up knowing very little about the entire set of strategic flows that drive their performance. Linkage analysis helps build integrated causal chains that enable organizations to connect more dots in their strategic mind space. As a result, when organizations embark upon these efforts, they tend to gain in one of two ways. They either verify their mental models by seeing them laid out and tested in their entirety or learn to challenge them by trying to reconcile them with what the data reveal. In either case, the net result is a model that data have either validated or challenged and that increases management's confidence level in whichever strategic route it chooses to follow.

Understanding Strategic Flows

As discussed earlier, the impact of pulling a strategic lever is often complicated and cascades through to its ultimate effect through a number of complex relationships. An absence of linkage analyses forces managers to make assumptions about these relationships. For example, an organization might change its innovation strategy from incremental innovation to radical innovation. This single change may have far-reaching consequences and affect the operations of the organization and the performance metrics in a variety of ways. Without the aid of an appropriate tool, it would be impossible for the managers or leaders of the organization to comprehend or measure the effects of changing the innovation philosophy. Linkage analyses provide the set of tools that would help management understand the "flow" from cause to effect through the various intervening relationships. They also measure the direction and size of these effects and help test both intuitive and formal hypotheses.

Exploiting Data Explosion

Because linkage analysis is data driven, it tends to put vast warehouses of data at organizations to good use. As was discussed earlier, many organizations are sitting on a goldmine of data from various sources including customers, employees, core operations, and financial operations. In many cases, these data are residing in various functional silos and few understand the power from integrating them. Linkage analysis provides a platform to break these silos, connect data from various functional areas, build cross-functional models, and discover the true drivers of firm performance. To that extent, linkage analyses help leverage the power of existing data and connect the dots to build strategic pictures on a larger canvas.

Uncovering Strategic Fulcrums

While many relationships or linkages may connect organizational actions to outcomes, we often find that actions directed at a small improvement in one metric or linkage relationship result in a large improvement in the performance of the ultimate outcome. In some firms, the key action is surrounding key hires, while in others it is retaining key core customers. In some, it relates to maintaining the equity of the key brand, and in others at maintaining a cost advantage on a key raw material. We refer to these critical metrics or relationships as the *strategic fulcrums* for the terminal outcome. Small changes around the strategic fulcrum result in large changes in performance. In other words, we can imagine the organization's success to pivot around is strategic fulcrums. The correct management of metrics around a strategic fulcrum has a high magnification effect on the organization's fate. Consequently, these fulcrums should be the locus of strategic activity.

In our experience, however, while several firms intuitively recognize that certain variables or factors matter more than others, virtually none does a complete analysis to discover its true strategic fulcrums. None tracks the movement of linkages to assess how strategic fulcrums evolve over time. For example, when oil prices are high, decisions related to hedging future oil purchases were critical for airlines because the cost of fuel emerged as a strategic fulcrum for relative competitiveness and profitability. The overall strategic impact of the hedge was more than just the cost savings on fuel. The linkages from the decision to hedge possibly related to pricing power, relative customer demand, load factors, revenues, and margins. However, if oil prices come down, the management of fuel prices may not remain a critical strategic fulcrum for any airline.

Similarly, lower distribution costs from a direct-to-customer distribution model might be a strategic fulcrum if the price-to-weight ratio of an electronic or a computer product is high but might not remain so when the ratio comes down. We find that organizations get trapped in legacy strategy systems because they do not explicitly identify their strategic fulcrums and do not track the evolution of fulcrums over time. Linkage analyses facilitate the discovery of these strategic fulcrums and the evaluation of the impact of managing them appropriately.

Building a Repository of Strategic Linkages

Finally, linkage analysis helps an organization build a repository of webs of linkages. For example, once the analysis is completed, the estimated relationships among the set of key linkages become a unit of learning that can be stored explicitly as part of a repository. At later points in time, the organization can draw upon these sets of linkages to estimate or predict the likely consequences from actions taken at future dates. For example, if an organization builds a repository of linkages that capture the effects of automating people-driven manual operations, it can better predict the outcome of future automation based on the learning embedded in previous linkages.

CHAPTER 8

The Decision Equity Metric

Operationalization

Operationalizing Decision Equity:
The Importance of Flowprinting

One of the most common challenges associated with the operationalization of decision equity pertains to what statisticians refer to as "model misspecification." Here is an easy example to illustrate the point. Let us think of two cardiologists, each of whom has very favorable perceptions of drug A—a statin used to lower cholesterol among patients. When the pharmaceutical company approached these physicians through a survey, they each reported very favorable perceptions of drug A, the company's sales force, as well as the company itself. However, the scripting data found very different scripting levels between these two cardiologists. One of them wrote twice as many absolute scripts or prescriptions for drug A compared to the other. Could the model be missing something—because it seems unlikely that two physicians with similar drug perceptions can engage in very different scripting behaviors? If the observed relationship between perceptions and behavior is missing some other critical source of information that can explain such discordance, then the current model is perhaps misspecified. Such misspecification can have serious implications on estimates of decision equity. For instance, if the firm were to invest in an advertising strategy to better communicate the benefits of the drug to cardiologists, then should it use the scripting behavior of the first or the second physician as the baseline case, or should it average the two?

We recently encountered a very similar situation. The decision makers were interested in initiating a promotional campaign to better communicate the efficacy, and the minimal side effects of their drug, and wanted to measure the decision equity associated with these promotional investments. However, they saw evidence similar to the one described above, wherein there seemed to be a weak relationship between physician perceptions of the drug—which was to be enhanced through the promotional campaign—and their scripting behavior. As we worked through the issue and developed it during the flowprinting sessions, four very important considerations emerged.

First, there was internal evidence in the organization that the years of experience with drug A can influence the volume of scripts written by the cardiologist. Earlier research had shown that as doctors gain more experience with the drug, their propensity to write a script for it increases. Therefore, it was possible that the difference in scripting behavior across physicians might be driven by their experience with the drug, and while there was little that the drug manufacturer could do to influence this driver of scripting, it had an important implication for the firm. Second, it was also hypothesized, with good empirical support, that the patient mix of each cardiologist can influence their scripting behavior of the drug, because clinical trials had shown drug A to work better with certain patient demographics. Therefore, even if two cardiologists had identical perceptions of the drug, and had similar years of experience with it, they could still exhibit very different scripting behaviors, based on their patient mix, which in turn might depend on the neighborhood where they practiced. A third consideration was simply the number of patients seen by each cardiologist. If some of them spend more time in research and less in actual clinical practice, then the number of scripts they write for the entire category of drugs might be lower vis-à-vis cardiologists who spend more time interacting with patients. Overall, we could have two physicians with similar perceptions and experiences with the drug and similar patient mixes who would differ in the number of scripts written for drug A, because they handled different volumes of patients. Last, but not the least, managed care—that is, the role of health insurance companies—also emerged as a very important consideration. While the two hypothetical physicians in our case study could be identical on all three criteria listed earlier, they each might be dealing with different managed care providers, and in the process have differential ease of access to drug A. This would have a substantial impact on the number of scripts they write for drug A (see Figure 8.1).

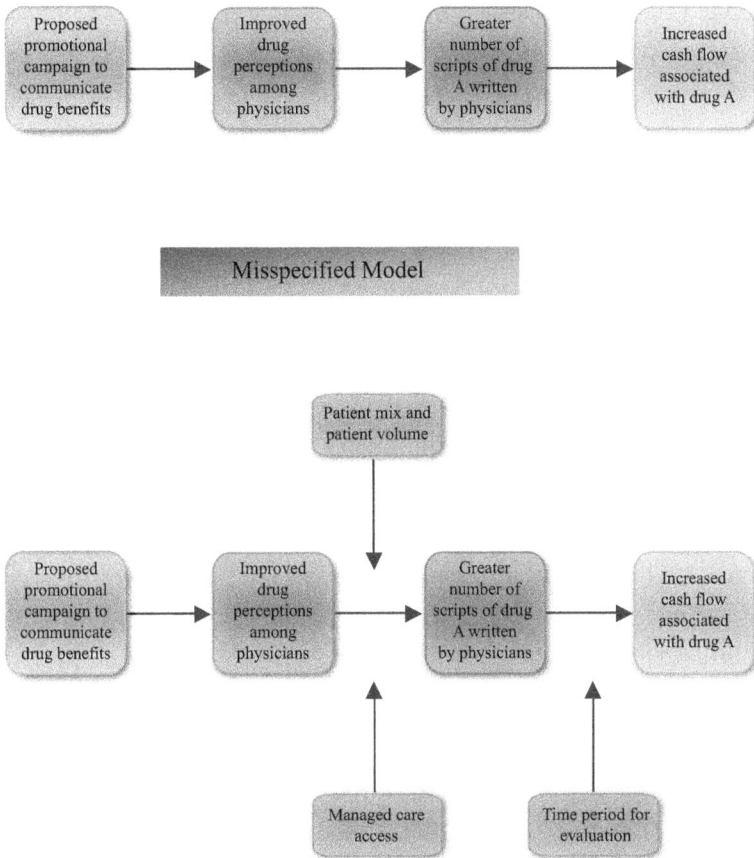

Figure 8.1. *Model misspecification.*

In our example, we could have computed decision equity relative to a baseline with or without model misspecification. A misspecified estimate would be one where we would study the investments in drug promotion, link them to improvements in physician perceptions of the drug, and then link such perceptual changes to scripting behavior, and eventually to the cash flows generated by these scripts over time. However, this would be a classic case of "model misspecification"—that is, an instance where we would have computed these relationships while ignoring many other important influencers that can affect the computation of the decision equity. Such misspecified models can provide estimates of decision equity that can be inflated or deflated, and there is no way to figure out the degree of error, unless other relevant influencers are included in the estimation. A more complete method would be one where measures on each relevant influencer are included in the model toward computing the decision equity of the proposed investment. In our case, this meant getting information on the number of years the cardiologist had been practicing as well as scripting drug A, information on their patient mix and volume, detailed data on managed care access for drug A as well as competing drugs. With the inclusion of all these factors, the estimates of the returns on investing in a drug promotional campaign were more accurate and had greater acceptance among the stakeholders.

The main thesis of this discussion is that the operationalization of the decision equity metric requires a deep understanding of the linkages among the many moveable parts that can influence, or be influenced by, a proposed decision. Organizations and decision makers need to avoid model misspecification, or else the strength of the estimated relationships in the flowprints will be biased, and the exercise will not generate a buy-in from internal champions. We find that misspecification can be avoided largely through careful thought and investments in the up-front flowprinting session. As discussed earlier, two key benefits of flowprinting are (a) recognition of the relationships among the various interconnected and nonstatic organizational silos and (b) a buy-in from relevant decision makers in these silos. The ability to draw from the experience of such decision makers in a flowprint session and in the process minimize the odds of excluding important measures, helps achieve both these objectives. In all our decision equity engagements, we increasingly insist on the need to have the right audience for the flowprint session. We also insist that the firm invest serious energy in designing a model that has face validity among executives, and one that does not exclude any important variable in the estimation of the decision equity metric. The job of the analyst is to then collate the relevant data related to these connected parts, and explore the linkages among them. When these results are presented to the decision makers, the research team essentially repeats the story line that was articulated in the flowprinting session, but with validation from real data. The flowprinting process also adds confidence to the estimates of decision equity, based on a more thorough evaluation of the measures that need to be incorporated in the models.

The need to minimize the exclusion of critical factors from the models requires careful discussion around at least three points. We have observed that these are applicable across industries and that while their individual importance might vary across contexts, their relevance does not.

Coverage of Multiple Domains

As we have noted earlier, the flowprints associated with a single strategic choice can be complex and run through multiple functional domains. The computation of decision equity requires an assessment of the cumulative changes in the costs, revenues, and cash flows associated with each domain and their integration into a single decision equity measure. For example, a large utility provider was exploring the concept of integrated customer centricity. Previously, the senior management of the firm received multiple resource allocation requests that were in line with the concept but were scattered and unrelated to each other. These included requests for more feet on the street for repair, greater investments in weather forecasting technology, investments for more power, and uniform load. However, the president of the company asked everyone to step back and explore the notion of customer centricity from an integrated perspective. Such an approach would give him an overarching equity value associated with implementing the concept. The subsequent evaluation of both residential and business customers provided a comprehensive list of touch points ranging from tree trimming to moving-in experience, and from call center interactions to billing perceptions. The estimation of the equity relating to the decision of being customer centric therefore necessitated an evaluation of the costs and revenues across multiple marketing, operations, and customer service domains, and ultimately led to an integrated and unified approach to selecting a portfolio of actions.

Importance of Time

Because changes in future cash flows form the basis of the computation of decision equity, it is important to calibrate what future really means. Often the specification of the time frame that constitutes the future has an impact on whether equity turns out to be favorable or not, and whether a decision appears worth making. For example, a financial institution we worked with undertook serious cost cutting measures to boost its profits. One of these cost containment measures came from its retail operations and resulted in a decline in the number of tellers at each branch. The bank also started charging a fee for certain services that were free until then.

Not long thereafter, customers began noticing the reduction in the number of tellers, the increased length of waiting lines, and the higher fee structure. Because other competing banks had not undertaken similar measures, customers began defecting in search of lower fees and better service. The customer satisfaction tracking system alerted management to the drop in satisfaction scores. However, many scoffed at the new numbers and pointed to the inverse relationship between increasing profits and falling satisfaction scores. Some even argued that the satisfaction numbers were perhaps wrong. In any case, if the equity associated with the decision to reduce the number of tellers and increase the fees was computed using a relatively short time frame, it would have looked positive and would have supported the decision that was made. The cost savings from the actions were virtually instantaneous while the revenue impact from customer defections would have unfolded over a longer time horizon. However, over the course of the next few months, the impact of the cost savings dried up and the revenue loss from customer defections overwhelmed the bank. As expected, the equity associated with the original decision did not look positive over this longer time horizon.

We observe similar time dependencies across many markets. Some consequences of a decision have a financial impact in very short periods while others unfold over a longer time horizon. For example, in the case of a computer hardware products company, we found differences from similar actions even across customer segments. In this case, the benefit of a positive action within the household segment was observed 3 to 4 years after the initial purchase, typically, when the household went in for a repurchase. However, the effects showed up in a matter of weeks for a small business. Finally, for large businesses, some benefits from service showed some up on a continuous basis in addition to large benefits that materialized only at the time of contract renewal. It is therefore important for firms to be sensitive to time frames when computing decision equity or acting on equity-driven choices. One approach to addressing this problem is to do scenario analyses with varying time frames. Managers can then evaluate the sensitivity of the decision equity to differences in time frames and assess the risk inherent in their decision.

Multiple Terminal Measures

While we have conceptualized decision equity in terms of the present value of incremental future cash flows associated with a decision, we find that firms are often more comfortable working with more traditional metrics that they are used to. For example, managers of the insurance firm that we alluded to earlier were more comfortable with their traditional "top line" versus "bottom line" measures of revenue and margins than with an integrated decision equity measure. Very often, a firm's ability to compute decision equity as a cash flow or bottom-line metric is also constrained by nonavailability of such financial metrics at the individual customer level. In other cases, organizations prefer other metrics such as economic growth, profit growth, or return on investments. Yet others use industry specific metrics, such as revenue per available room in the hospitality sector, or sales per square foot in the retail sector. However, while the migration to the most appropriate metric may take multiple steps, these firms nevertheless benefit enormously from the process of linkage analysis and discovering the relationships among alternative actions and their downstream consequences. The concept of decision equity is still very applicable, and it is critical to remember that, irrespective of the choice of the downstream metric, decision makers are ultimately interested in the ability to compare noncomparable actions using some common set of measures.

Options for Operationalizing Decision Equity

We conceptualize decision equity in terms of the present value of the future incremental cash flows that result from a managerial decision. While the underlying premise of this concept may be familiar, appealing, and powerful, its implementation is often not as simple or straightforward. This should not come as a surprise because the range of strategic decisions and the flowprints of their downstream consequences vary significantly across industries, firms, and over time. In each case, one of the early questions that comes up is the definition of the benchmark relative to which the value of decision equity will be computed. In other words, as a firm prepares to implement a new action plan and wishes to measure the cash flows attributable to that decision, the question always is what reference level should it use to estimate the benefit it can achieve from the proposed implementation?

In our experience, there are typically two options available to decision makers. The first is adopting the status quo as a benchmark. This approach sets up the floor for the computation of decision equity under the assumption that doing nothing would result in no incremental changes in the ultimate outcomes and would therefore have decision equity of zero. The second option is to compare the decision equity associated with a particular action plan with equities associated with similar other action plans that might be implemented. This way, decision makers can estimate the equities associated with multiple decisions, and then compare and evaluate them on common downstream metrics.

Estimating Decision Equity Relative to the Status Quo

The easiest way to understand the status quo approach is to go back to the flowprint discussion earlier in the chapter, and imagine that none of the interconnected parts is undergoing any movement from the current state. In other words, everything that the organization did in the previous time period will continue to operate identically, and continue to provide some downstream results. Now imagine that the decision maker decides to make a change to a particular area of performance. As a result, much like a series of gears connected to each other, the change will generate movement in the web of relationships. This movement will eventually move the final node of the web, the chosen downstream metric, in a positive or negative direction, by a certain magnitude. The change in intermediate markers throughout the web of relationships, and eventually in the downstream measure, such as cash flow, can then be evaluated over a period of time to estimate the equity associated with the change.

When the status quo is a benchmark, it is important to recognize that if a decision maker alters one node, it is unreal to expect everything else to stay the same. For instance, if a firm invests in improved distribution of its product, competition might undertake an action, such as price reduction, which can influence the focal firm's effort to increase market penetration through increased distribution. A model generated through a comprehensive flowprint will account for these consequential or conditional effects and not assume that the world would not respond to an action chosen. In our example, the firm would perhaps need to account for a potential price drop by a competitor when estimating the decision equity associated with the change in its own distribution.

Under this approach, we assume that the current state of affairs or the status quo represents the starting point. If an action results in an incremental increase in future cash flows, then there would be some positive decision equity associated with it. In other words, decision equity is measured as the incremental change in the present value of the future cash flows resulting from an action. The challenge is establishing both the starting point and the change resulting from the action under consideration. A part of the reason for the challenge is that most managers and executives do not have information on the cash flows associated with the status quo, and do not necessarily plan with cash flows as a primary metric. However, it can be computed at the start of a linkage analysis project.

In order to delve deeper into this issue, let us consider the case of a leading property and casualty insurer in the United States. The firm was performing relatively well and was aspiring to grow very aggressively. However, management was unsure whether future growth would come more from acquiring new customers or increasing the rate of retention among existing ones. Field agents strongly influenced customer management at this firm, and were, in turn, influenced by the structure of their bonus payments. The bonus computation and agent ranking system that was in place at the firm for a long time was designed with customer acquisition in mind. It rewarded agents with strong acquisition capabilities and therefore promoted an acquisition-centric culture across the organization. However, over time, the pool of available customers shrank, and the firm was forced to review its customer management strategy. The new strategic thinking gave more weight to retention than the previous mind-set.

The finance department of the firm weighed in on the strategic decision to shift from customer acquisition to customer retention. However, in its assessment, the impact of the new customer orientation was contingent on which metric was to be used to make the strategic call. Continuing with an acquisition focused strategy was still a superior alternative from a revenue or premium perspective. However, retention seemed to be more promising from a margin or profit perspective because the cost of acquiring customers at this firm was more than that of retaining them.

Now because this firm had an existing acquisition-oriented customer management program, the current practice and the cash flows resulting from it would be considered the status quo or the starting point. The identifiable strategic shift was the decision to switch from an acquisition orientation to a retention orientation. The specific action associated with this intended shift was a change in the compensation structure of the field agents. The change could result in a rise or fall in the cash flow stream generated because of changes in customer margins, retention versus acquisition costs, bonus payments, and other cash costs. The discounted present value of these *incremental* changes would therefore constitute the decision equity related to the strategic action of switching from customer acquisition to customer retention, and altering the bonus structure for field agents. On the other hand, if the management of the firm were to choose to continue with its customer management strategy, there would be no equity associated the strategic choice because it did not deviate from the status quo. In this case, the analysis revealed that the switch from an acquisition to a retention orientation would have resulted in net positive decision equity because of higher margins and smaller customer management costs. Consequently, the firm realized that the current strategy of revenue growth was coming at the expense of profitability and made the switch toward the new orientation.

Now as an aside, let us imagine what would happen to the customers of the firm following the decision to switch the customer management strategy. The firm's customer base could possibly shrink relative to what it would have been under the existing system. It is also possible that the value of each of the remaining customers would be higher than what it was under the current environment of high customer churn rates under an acquisition oriented strategy. The question we should ask ourselves is whether there was a change in the lifetime value of the firm's individual customers and their collective customer equity. In other words, did the customer equity go up or down? The answer in this case could be that the average lifetime value of the remaining customers would perhaps be higher than before. However, it could very well be the other way around in a different context. The important question however is whether the equity associated with a proposed action is positive or not. The lifetime value of the customers is a consequence or a beneficiary of the action and should be a secondary consideration. It may go up for some high equity decisions and may go down for others. However, in either case, customers are not the residence of the change in equity.

Estimating Decision Equity Relative to Other Options

In reality though, an organization has multiple decision makers and functional areas, and each of them is constantly making changes, small or large, in their daily operations as well as their strategic plans. From a flowprint perspective, one can imagine that the web of relationships among actions and consequences is constantly changing. In the world of pharmaceutical manufacturers for example, three plans might be implemented simultaneously. The sales team might invest in initiatives that can increase sales force knowledge of the drug as well as the therapeutic category. The brand team might invest in new promotional materials. Finally, the managed care team might work on improving physician access to the drug under various health insurance plans. Each of these decisions will have an influence on the cash flow of the organization, and under a properly specified model we can estimate them fairly accurately. The relative equities of each of these decisions can then be compared to identify the one with the greatest potential.

In our experience, this particular method of estimating decision equity seems to be the most prevalent. Decision makers are often interested in estimating the financial returns associated with alternate investment options, and juxtaposing them next to each other on common downstream metrics. Such comparisons are often done using simulators, wherein decision makers use information derived from robust statistical analysis, and couple it with their experience to estimate the equity of multiple decisions. The ability to compare them on a common metric, such as the future cash flows, makes the comparison more equitable. While some inputs to these estimations might not be completely scientific, such as the selected time period over which the proposed benefit will accrue, the analyses still offer very valuable guidance to decision makers when comparing alternate and hitherto noncomparable investment decisions.

Case Study: Estimating Decision Equity Relative to Other Options

A retail bank had undertaken an initiative to improve the quality of its in-branch transactions. In an environment where other banks were encouraging their customers to stay away from the branch and use web-based and automated teller machine–based services, this organization decided to invest in providing top-notch experiences to customers that visited its branches. The location and demographic mix of its customer base justified such thinking. To provide such quality transactions, an option that was under serious consideration was the increase in the number of tellers in targeted branches during peak traffic hours in order to minimize the wait time for the customers. As shown in Figure 8.2, the increased number of tellers was estimated to reduce the average wait time for customers in these branches by about 2 minutes, which, based on an earlier model, was expected to increase customer satisfaction with the in-branch experience by an average of 10%. Improved transactional satisfaction, in turn, had been modeled to provide a series of downstream benefits—more favorable overall customer affinity toward the bank (+5%), ability to lock in greater share of deposits (+10%) and loans (+20%) from each household, and a consequent increase in cash flow per household ($100).[1] Across all the households that were retail customers of these branches of the bank, the discounted value of the net increase in cash flows over 3 years was projected to be to the tune of $100 million. The bank also estimated a cash outlay of about $20 million for the hiring, training, and remuneration of the additional tellers over the same time period, resulting in a net incremental cash flow of $80 million.

Around the time this decision was ready to be implemented, another stream of internal research pointed to an alternative strategy. Specifically, it pointed out that an increase in the performance-based compensation structure of the existing tellers would lead to a similar chain of effects

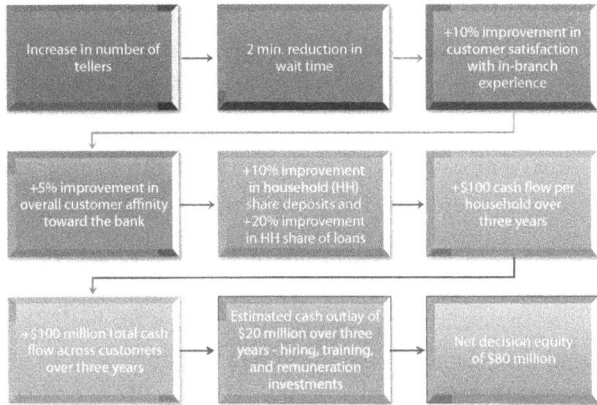

Option 1. Increasing the number of tellers.

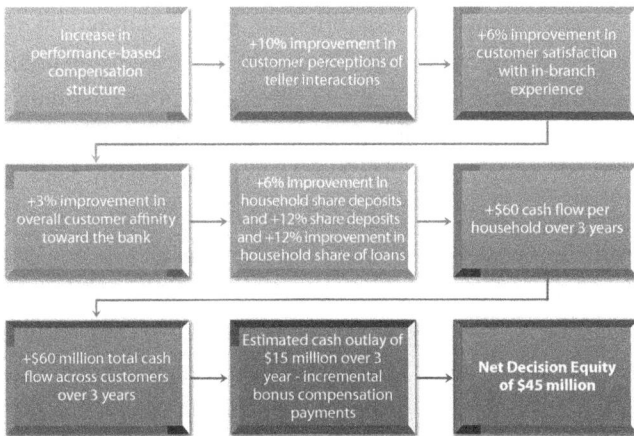

Option 2. Changing the compensation structure.

Figure 8.2. Case study: Estimating decision equity relative to other options.

or flowprint (Figure 8.2). The structure of such compensation change would motivate the employees to be more customer centric in their interactions with the customers, leading to a 10% improvement in customer perceptions of teller interactions and a 6% improvement in satisfaction with their overall in-branch experience. The increased satisfaction, in turn, would lead to about a 3% improvement in overall customer affinity toward the bank. The subsequent downstream impacts of such improvement in affinity would be similar—greater share of loans (+6%) and deposits (+12%), incremental cash flow per household (+$60), totaling up to an incremental cash flow of $60 million across the customer base over 3 years. The cash outlay associated with the change in compensation structure was estimated to be $15 million, generating a net decision equity of approximately $45 million.

As the decision makers evaluated the two options, they were able to account for the cash flows and decision equities for both on a common metric and time frame. There was some trepidation around a permanent increase in the number of employees on the payroll, vis-à-vis a more flexible compensation structure change for the current employees. Ultimately, the executives favored the first option and accepted it for implementation.

From an organizational learning perspective, the decision makers acquired knowledge about four important issues during this process. One, the flowprint exercise helped them link various moving parts of the overall customer experience that had till then been studied only within individual silos. For example, the exercise helped them recognize the linkages among employee compensation and engagement, length of in-branch wait time, quality of in-branch customer experience, overall affinity toward the bank, share of loans and deposits, and incremental cash flows. Until then, each of these measures was studied in isolation, without recognizing how they are all connected in a web of close relationships. Two, developing this big picture helped them gather a strategic perspective of their business, and of the linkages among various metrics. Now for instance, they could quantify the benefit of an increase in employee engagement in dollars and cents, instead of simply tracking it as a standalone metric and feeling good about it moving northward. The human resource team could now go to management and make a business case for employee-centric investments. Three, the decision makers were able to compare two very different decisions, that were each designed to provide the same ultimate outcome, on a common metric. In the absence of the decision equity approach, these two decisions were non comparable, and management might have acted on their intuition in selecting one over the other. Finally, the learning set a great precedent for future decision making. Management could now share a case study with functional heads, to showcase the process they should undertake to justify their resource needs by linking functional decisions to the organizational bottom line. It also encouraged functional managers to appreciate the linkages among cross-functional intermediate markers, and recognize that an upward change in these markers—including their own functional metrics—was useful only as far as its ability to link to the final desired measure of financial success.

Confidence in Decision Equity Comparisons

The ability to confidently compare alternate investment options, such as the two cited in the previous case study, is contingent on other important considerations. From a process perspective, two salient inputs that inspire confidence are the development of a comprehensive flowprint and the availability of reliable and valid data to *breathe life into the flowprint*. The inability to meet either of these two criteria can cast serious doubts on the quality of decision support provided by the decision equity approach. It is therefore critical that managers invest enough time in the up-front design phase toward developing a relevant flowprint, and gathering the required data. Managerial inputs on investments required also play an important role in the comparison of the decision equity metrics associated with the alternate investment decisions. These resources could relate to the monetary investments, time constraints, as well as other inputs. For example, if the cash outlay for hiring more tellers were $60 million versus the estimated $20 million in the case study discussed previously, the chosen option would be very different. Similarly, if management was interested in a 1-year versus a 3-year time frame, the chosen action plan could have been different. Last, but not the least, nonmathematical strategic considerations may often override the considerations highlighted by the estimation of the decision equity metric. For example, if the equity estimates recommend acting on a certain performance domain, but organizational legacy forbids managers to make investments in that area, then management might select an alternate option despite lower equity. Overall, the computation of decision equity relative to the status quo is conceptually closest to the definition of the construct. Therefore, wherever possible, we try to embrace this approach to estimate its value. However, more often than not, we run into either composite decisions or management's desire to test multiple but a limited number of options in one shot. In such cases, we use data analysis tools to parse out the decision equity associated with each of the individual choices. Management then makes an informed call regarding the decisions to continue with and those that need to be dropped. We rarely see a bake-off among many independent decisions and rank ordering them based on their respective equities. However, the equity estimation serves as a powerful tool to compare non-comparable options on a common ultimate metric, and in conjunction with other strategic considerations, leads to well-informed, data-driven choices. When done right, the decision equity–driven approach is a vastly superior alternative to intuition-based decision making.

PART III

Pursuing Excellence Through Decision Equity

CHAPTER 9

A Best Practice Approach to Linkage Analysis

A Framework for Conducting Linkage Analysis

The prospect of linking metrics across functional areas is an exciting but challenging exercise. Hasty or analytically weak decisions can unfortunately lead to severe adverse consequences. For instance, a bank that reduces the number of tellers in its branches as a cost cutting measure will likely experience erosion of customer loyalty because of increased waiting time at the branches. In the short term, however, despite eroding customer loyalty, profits might go up, largely because of the cost reduction measures undertaken by the bank. The link between customer loyalty and the financial performance of the firm might thus seem negative in the short run, thereby challenging the wisdom for cross-functional linkages. This negative relationship will however correct itself over time, as more unhappy customers defect to other banking institutions, leading to reduced profits. The ability to link these data will then provide an early indication of the long-term risk exposure of the bank, and allow the bank to take proactive corrective actions. Such examples bring to light the onus associated with performing linkage analyses, and the need for a systematic and rigorous approach to establishing the hypothesized links.

Significant challenge also comes from the infancy of research on conducting such linkage analyses. The few studies documented in the academic world are less constrained by time and other resources. In the applied world, however, resource limitations are more real. The ability to work within a given budgetary and time constraint is critical in business world applications, introducing greater pressures to perform the analyses within the limited resources. In view of the aforementioned challenges and potential pitfalls, the need to adopt a systematic and rigorous approach to linkage analysis that is also sensitive to the resource limitations suggests the need for following a best-practice approach to performing these analyses. Therefore, we present a 10-step approach for linking various measures of organizational performance. To provide an easy-to-follow framework, we present a case where attitudinal measures of customer loyalty are linked to measures of customer behavior and downstream financial results. The implications of the framework however apply to all sorts of organizational data.

The proposed approach offers four key benefits: First, it allows the parties engaging in linkage analyses to evaluate the need for, and benefits of, undertaking linkage analyses. Second, it allows them to gauge their readiness for conducting linkage analyses by getting a better understanding of resource requirements for successful completion of the project. Third, it sensitizes linkage analysts to some of the common pitfalls encountered during the analytical process. Finally, the proposed framework allows easy customization for adaptation to various industry and marketplace environments. Past research has shown that a variety of factors, such as the degree of competition, market cycle, consumption cycles, and formality of the buyer-seller relationship can all influence the appropriateness and viability of these links. Our approach is sensitive to the need for customization, and thus refrains from proposing a standard one-size-fits-all approach. Instead, it provides a framework, individual components of which can be customized to suit the needs of a specific project.

The Proposed Ten-Step Filtration Process

The best practice approach described here is the outcome of learning accumulated over multiple linkage projects, across organizations in different industries, allowing us to draw from the common observations across these studies. Such an overview has led us to conclude that the ability to conduct successful linkage analyses is both an "art" and a "science." We hope to bring forth this sensitivity and recognition in this section of the book. We propose that the ability to conduct successful linkage analysis is contingent on its ability to pass through a sequence of filters that represent varying shades of art and science required for success in this domain. An inability of the analyses to pass through a particular filter reduces the probability of success in subsequent steps. Each filter thus affects the probability of success in subsequent steps of the project. Overall, the proposed best practice approach lists and discusses 10 such filters (Figure 9.1). We provide a theoretical rationale as well as empirical

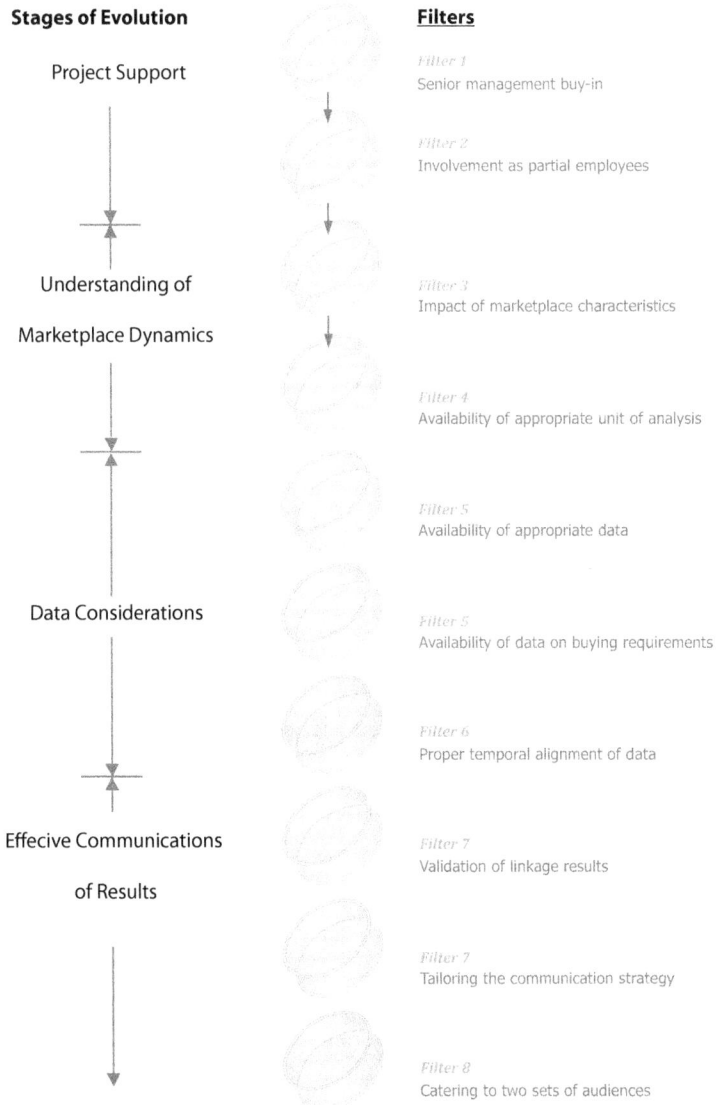

Stages of Evolution	Filters
Project Support	Filter 1 Senior management buy-in
	Filter 2 Involvement as partial employees
Understanding of Marketplace Dynamics	Filter 3 Impact of marketplace characteristics
	Filter 4 Availability of appropriate unit of analysis
	Filter 5 Availability of appropriate data
Data Considerations	Filter 5 Availability of data on buying requirements
	Filter 6 Proper temporal alignment of data
Effecive Communications of Results	Filter 7 Validation of linkage results
	Filter 7 Tailoring the communication strategy
	Filter 8 Catering to two sets of audiences

Figure 9.1. The 10-step filtration process.

support for these filters through real-life case studies. In addition, we discuss these filters along the chronological evolution of the project—that is, from early on in the process to its conclusion. While some of these can be more salient in certain environments, we have experienced that each of them is important in its own way. The sequencing of the filters and the relative importance of each of them can however vary across industries, requiring appropriate customization of the proposed approach. And to reiterate, while the framework here is presented within the context of linking customer attitudes to customer behavior and financial activity data, the discussion is equally applicable for linkages among other key organizational metrics.

At a higher level, the 10 filters we discuss here toward linking attitudinal perceptions of individual customers, to their behavior and financial activity can be organized along four broad themes: *project support, understanding of marketplace dynamics, data considerations, and effective communication of results* (Figure 9.1). By their basic nature, linkage analyses frequently involve active interaction between the sponsoring and the research organization, as well as between multiple units of the sponsoring organization. This necessitates the need for adequate *project support*, and these needs are discussed in filters one and two of the proposed best-practice approach. Linkage analyses also require business managers to revisit their *understanding of the marketplace dynamics* to gauge the viability and appropriateness of undertaking efforts to perform the analyses. The issues related to marketplace dynamics are discussed in the third and fourth filters. If adequate project support and the appropriateness of marketplace dynamics are estimated successfully, the next stage of evolution relates to *data considerations* for performing the analyses. These are multiple data requirements that require thoughtful consideration for linkage analysis, and these are discussed along fifth, sixth, and seventh filters of the framework. Finally, because of the infancy of such analyses in the applied world, even rigorous linkage efforts are often viewed skeptically, or with lack of interest—if the results are not communicated effectively. *Effective communication of results* is thus discussed as the last of the four stages of evolution, and specific issues related to communication of results are discussed in the last 3 filters of the 10-step filtration process.

Project Support

Filter 1: Senior Management Buy-In

Linking customer perceptions to actual customer behavior and bottom-line data typically involves the coming together of different functions of the sponsoring firm. For instance, a key requirement for performing linkage analyses is the availability of customer perception data, and the financial activity data for such customers. Typically, the customer data resides with the marketing (research) department of the firm, and the financial data with the accounting or the finance department. More often than not, these departments work isolated from each other and zealously guard the data that reside within their control. Working collaboratively on linkage analysis therefore requires a cultural shift for the departments, which more often than not, is met with resistance.

In such environments, if support for the proposed linkage analysis comes from the very top in the organization, it provides an impetus to these departments to share their data and their learning in a collaborative manner. When the mandate does not come from the very top, and worse when the leaders of the organization do not share the motivation for linkage analysis, the exercise gets challenging. Inordinate amounts of time and resources then need to be spent to elicit the basic information required for analyses. In most of the successful linkage assignments that we have conducted, the interest, the motivation, and the buy-in for linkage have come from very senior managers that have high levels of vested authority. In one project, it was the chief operating officer (COO) of a large financial organization, in another it was the president of a utility company, and in yet another, a senior C-level executive in a health-care organization. All these senior managers were convinced about linking cross-functional performance metrics, and their buy-in and sponsorship made it easier to elicit the cooperation of different people and divisions within each of these companies to work toward a common goal.

Filter 2: Willingness of Sponsoring Individuals to Act as Active Participants

Unlike many other research programs, linkage analysis, by its basic nature, is a highly interactive process that involves frequent communication and exchange of information between the sponsoring and the research firm. For instance, a good strategy to kick off the project is to have a flowprint meeting between the sponsoring firm and the linkage research and analysis team. Such a meeting allows business managers to detail the links that they expect to see in their marketplace, and allows the research analysts to translate such links into potential relationships to be explored in the data. Similar engagements from managers of the sponsoring organization are important throughout the process, requiring significant time commitments from these individuals over the span of the analysis. The success of linkage projects is therefore contingent on the commitment of business managers to act as active participants during the life of the project. And from a process perspective, it becomes important to set realistic expectations early on in the process about the involvement and role of relevant individuals from the sponsoring firm for the successful completion of the linkage exercise.

In our experience, it helps to detail the expected involvement of individuals from the sponsoring firm by flowcharting the overall process of the linkage project. One such example that was used in an engagement is presented in Figure 9.2. The flowchart of the process clearly identifies the interim points where active participation of individuals from the sponsoring firm is sought, allowing these individuals to recognize the importance of their participation toward successful completion of the overall project. We have consistently experienced that involvement from required individuals, if obtained effortlessly, contributes immensely to the success of linkage projects.

Understanding of Marketplace Dynamics

Filter 3: Understanding the Impact of Marketplace Characteristics on the Strength of the Link

Customer loyalty research posits that customers with more favorable attitudes exhibit more favorable behavior, which in turn provides financial benefits to the firm. It is however important to recognize that this

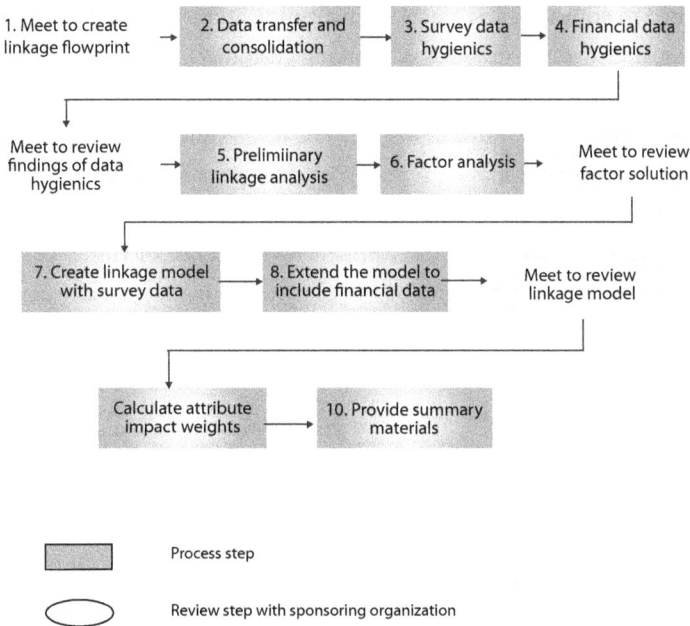

Figure 9.2. Flowcharting the research process.

relationship is not ubiquitous. Instead, the presence of a positive link between customer perceptions of the firm and their behavior is contingent on certain marketplace characteristics. Therefore, these characteristics must be understood before the customer-financial linkage analysis is attempted in order to gauge the viability of such analyses. In general, a positive link between customer perceptions and their behavior is observed in markets where customers can freely act on their perceptions and attitudes. Therefore, a positive link can be expected in markets where dissatisfied customers can easily defect to alternate suppliers without incurring significant monetary or psychological costs related to such defection. By way of contrast, in other environments, where customers are unable to act as freely on their perceptions of the firm, the presence as well as the strength of the positive link may not be strong. For instance, in order to avoid monetary penalties for breach of contract, unhappy customers might continue to do business with the firm even though these customers may be motivated to seek alternatives. Similarly, in environments characterized by psychological costs associated with defection, such as the effort required to educate a new financial institution about all the complex borrowing and investment needs of banking customers, dissatisfied customers may not defect. Further, for certain basic goods and services, increased customer spending with the firm may be less a function of their loyalty toward the firm and more a function of their personal needs. For example, utility consumption will be related to the size of a customer's residence and family structure (e.g., presence vs. absence of young children at home), rather than how happy the customer is with a service provider. In such environments, a positive link between customer perceptions and behavior can be expected to be weak or missing.

Interestingly, in work we have done for some industries, where the exit barriers are high for customers, we observe a negative link between customer attitudes and customer behavior. In working with a telecommunication provider, for example, we separated the data into two sets (Figure 9.3). The first of these data was for competitive geographies, wherein the customer was free to select their telecommunications provider. For this set of data, as should be expected, we did find a positive link between customer attitudes and behavior. Customers that reported more favorable attitudes toward the firm also exhibited more favorable behavior in terms of growth in their business with the firm. The other set of data was for geographies where the customers had very limited, if any, choice in selecting their telecommunication provider. For all practical purposes, the firm held a monopoly position in these second set of markets. When we studied the linkages between customer attitudes and customer behavior for this set of data, we were surprised to find a weak *negative* relationship. We observed that customers who reported less favorable attitudes actually exhibited higher absolute spends as well as higher growths in spends over the last few periods. However, subsequent investigation revealed that in the causality in such cases does not necessarily run from customer behavior to customer attitudes. Instead, customers who spend more with the firm are more likely to have higher expectations and therefore less likely to be satisfied. Thus, in such monopolistic situations, less favorable attitudes do not always lead to less favorable behaviors. Instead, more favorable behaviors may lead to less favorable attitudes.

For any proposed linkage analysis, it is therefore important to scope out the viability of the analysis by paying special attention to identifying

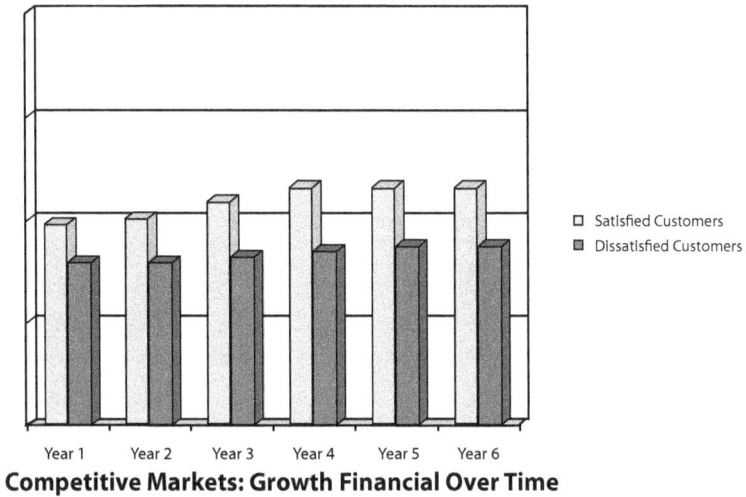

Competitive Markets: Growth Financial Over Time

Legend: Satisfied Customers / Dissatisfied Customers

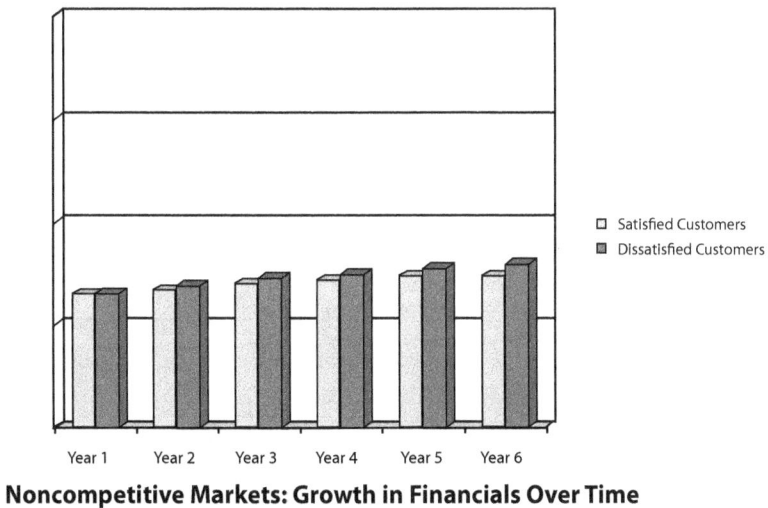

Noncompetitive Markets: Growth in Financials Over Time

Figure 9.3. Impact of marketplace dynamics.

the characteristics that define the marketplace that may affect any potential linkage between customer and financial measurements. In the telecommunication example discussed previously, for example, we used the
information to demonstrate the *financial opportunity at risk* in markets
that are still monopolistic. We looked at the financial vulnerability of
the company in monopoly markets when these markets were to become

competitive in the future. The approach helped reinforce the importance of delivering favorable customer experiences not only in competitive markets but also in the currently noncompetitive markets that could open to competition over the next few years.

Filter 4: Availability of an Appropriate Unit of Analysis

Customer perceptions can be meaningfully linked to customer behavior and other bottom-line data, but only if the market and data structures provide a meaningful unit of analysis to perform such linkages. This meaningful unit of analysis could be an individual customer, a household, a retail unit, a group of customers, a geographical region, or even points in time. For instance, for a company that sells its merchandise directly to the customer and has information on the perceptions and behavior of individual customers, an appropriate unit of analysis could be an individual customer. In these cases, individual customer loyalty toward the organization can be meaningfully linked to the financial contribution that each of these customers provides to the firm. In retail environments of hotels and banks, an individual franchise or property could also be treated as a meaningful unit of analysis, wherein the customer loyalty levels at each of these franchise or property levels can be meaningfully linked to the financial performance of these units.

Oftentimes, however, the choice of the unit of analysis is governed by the availability of data. In one recent business-to-business assignment for instance, we collected individual customer perceptions toward the firm from respondents located in various physical sites across the nation. Customer perception data were thus available at an individual site level, which in this study was our preferred unit of analysis. The financial data for these customers was however not available at the level of individual sites. Instead, as a historical practice, the customer activity and financial data were stored only at a regional level, with each region consisting of multiple sites. Thus while we collected customer perception data at the individual site level, our ability to use individual sites as units of analyses was restricted by the nonavailability of customer activity data for individual sites. We therefore modified our research agenda to select these regions as the unit of analysis, even though the choice led to two handicaps: (a) region-level data provided fewer data points to perform the customer-financial linkage analyses; and (b) the quality of data was compromised because individual site-level idiosyncrasies were ignored in aggregating the data to a regional level. The learning however provided stimulus to collect and record financial data for customers at the level of individual sites, to improve the quality of future analyses.

Data Considerations

Filter 5: Availability of Appropriate Data at the Chosen Unit of Analysis

Establishing a link between customer perceptions and downstream measures typically involves eliciting information from databases that may have little in common. It has been our experience that in some organizations the customer and financial databases evolve over time to cater solely to their primary users. The isolated evolution of these databases reduces their commonality and the ability to be linked. For example, the absence of a common customer identifier across the two databases can preclude linking individual customer perceptions to customer activity data, if an individual customer were the preferred unit of analysis. Likewise, the absence of certain financial data for all or some of the customers that report their perceptions to a survey instrument can limit the scope of the linkage analysis. On the other hand, certain survey research programs allow respondents anonymity because of the sociocultural environment or regulatory mandates in which these surveys are administered. When many respondents exercise their right to stay anonymous, the scope of the linkage analysis is curtailed, because these anonymous customers cannot be identified and their business activity levels cannot be determined.

Firms that practice a direct-to-customer business model typically possess better quality of data about their customers. The databases of these firms, by virtue of their business model, are better designed to record behavioral activities of individual customers. Also, by the nature of their business model, it is easier for these firms to furnish more accurate contact information about their customers to collect customer perceptions. For firms that do not follow a direct-to-customer business model, the quality of data about their customers is inversely related to the layers of intermediaries between the firm and the customer. The more separated the firm is from the end user, the lower is the likelihood that the firm will possess rich and reliable data about these users. Researchers thus need to be cognizant of any nonavailability or the inaccuracy of data to help scope their analysis. Such realizations often result in modifications to future data collection strategies, in order to perform the desired linkage analysis at a later point in time.

Filter 6: The Need to Have Information on Customer Buying Requirements

Assuming the linkage analysis effort has successfully passed through the first five filters, the research strategy should now begin to focus on some specific, microissues related to availability of appropriate data. The first of these issues relates to an understanding that in competitive markets, differences in the level of business activity of various customers of the firm is contingent on at least two key factors: differences in the level of loyalty of these customers and differences in the volume of their buying needs for the product category. One customer might thus buy more from a firm vis-à-vis another because this customer shares a greater sense of loyalty toward the firm, as well as because the customer has greater need for the product category in general. Differences in loyalty perceptions are typically gathered in the Customer Loyalty and Relationship Management (CLRM) program survey instruments through measures such as "overall satisfaction." However, by themselves, these measures may be insufficient for creating effective linkages between customer perceptions and customer behavior. Differences in the buying needs of individual customers should also be acknowledged to meaningfully link customer perceptions and behavior data.

In our experience, most firms undertaking linkage analyses projects do not acknowledge differences in buying needs of their customers while attempting to link customer perception and behavior data. Among firms that do recognize this need, either of two options is typically employed for collecting appropriate data. One, they ask respondents to report the volume of their total product category buying needs as a part of the survey. These self-reported buying needs are then used as proxies for the actual buying needs of these customers. Our experience tells us that generally customers are very forthcoming in sharing data on their total buying needs in a survey-based feedback environment. In sharing data on their buying needs and therefore allowing the firm to estimate a customer's share of business allocated to the firm, the customers want to send a clear message to the firm. In cases where the customer allocates a large share of their business, say 100%, the customer wants the firm to recognize the level of partnership they expect in reciprocation from the firm. On the other hand, where the current share-of-business allocated by the customer is small, it wants the firm to recognize the total potential available to the firm if it were to work harder in fostering a stronger relationship with the firm.

The other option available to a firm for estimating the buying needs of customers is through proxy variables such as the number of employees that work for the organization, or the total sales of the organization. For instance, the number of white-collar workers reported in a published secondary data source can be used as a proxy for the office stationary needs of the firm, while the square footage can be used as a proxy for the office furniture needs of the same firm. While each of these proxy measures are likely to have some error associated with them, in our experience, they provide a lot of useful information vis-à-vis the alternate option of not having the information at all. For example, in one linkage analysis that reported buying requirements estimated through the proxy method discussed previously, the link between the customer perceptions and behavior improved considerably when such information was included in the analysis (Figure 9.4).

Filter 7: Proper Temporal Alignment of Customer and Financial Data

Customers, in their role as information processors, process their recent experiences with a firm, form overall affective and cognitive attitudes based on these and past experiences, and then act on such attitudes at a future point in time. A satisfied customer will thus plan to continue doing business with a firm, while a dissatisfied customer might plan to defect at a future point in time. Meaningful linkage analysis should therefore have the perceptual and behavioral data that are properly aligned in time, with perceptual data preceding the behavioral data. Absence of the proper temporal alignment can influence the quality of linkage analyses. It has been our experience that most first-generation linkage analysis models commence with data that are not most appropriately aligned in time. These models are still able to demonstrate positive links between

Customer Perceptions and Behavior

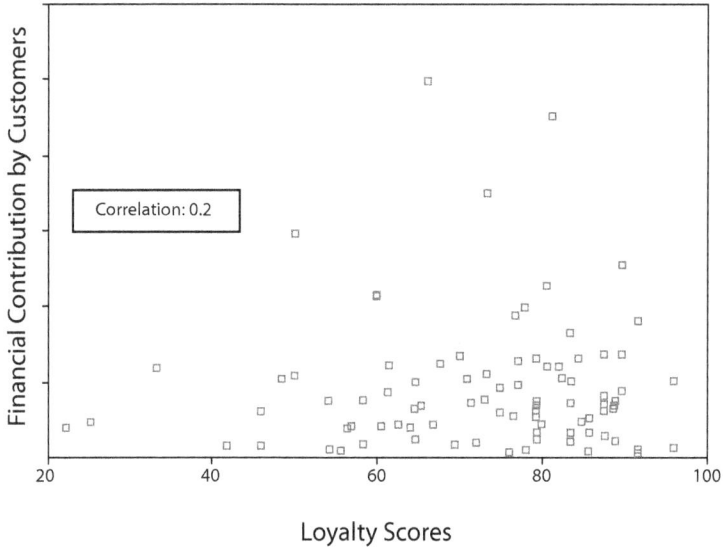

Without Controlling for Differences in Buying Requirements

Customer Perceptions and Behavior

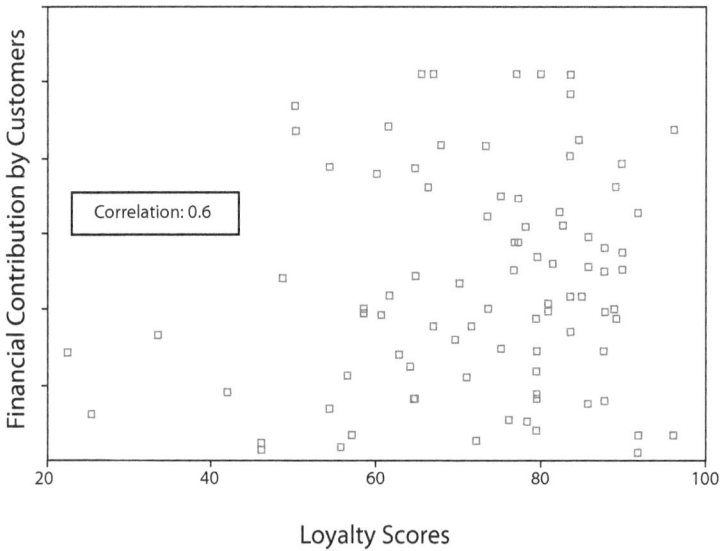

After Controlling for Differences in Buying Requirements

Figure 9.4. Incorporating buying size requirements.

customer perceptions and actual behavior, largely because in a mature marketplace, few customers change their behavior drastically over consecutive buying cycles. The linkage results of these first generation models, however, usually improve when customer perceptions are matched with future behavior data, because the alignment is more consistent with the decision-making processes of customers.

In a recent assignment, we performed the analysis with data that were cross-sectional, that is, where customer perceptions did not precede customer behavior that was reported in the data. Instead both the perceptions and behavior data came from the same period of time. Subsequently, we got an opportunity to monitor the behavior of these same customers over the next few months, and to reattempt the linkage analysis with the data that were more properly aligned—with this new behavioral data following the perceptual data in time. In this revised version of the model, the link from customer perceptions to their actual behavior improved significantly, validating the importance of proper temporal alignment of such data. We have similarly observed in other studies that when a link between customer perceptions and lagged customer behavior is attempted, it usually provides an improvement over comparable models that do not allow proper temporal alignment of data. While the amount of lag differs across industries, it should always be greater than or equal to the average buying cycle of the product category, to allow customers a subsequent buying opportunity to exhibit their (lack of) loyalty to the organization.

Effective Communication of Results

Filter 8: The Importance of Validating the Linkage Results

Because of the infancy of linkage analysis in the applied world, even a rigorous and carefully conducted analysis is often viewed skeptically. Business managers often continue to doubt the veracity of analyses that demonstrate links between "soft" customer attitudes and "hard" behavioral and financial data. One effective method to address such skepticism is to provide validation to the results of linkage analysis. For example, validation using a holdout sample can be a potent approach. In applying such an analytical strategy, a random portion of the total data is "safe-vaulted" for subsequent use. All initial linkage analyses are then per-formed on the remaining "main" portion of the data. Once these analy-ses are completed and a linkage model has been developed, the holdout sample is used to validate the findings. Specifically, the parameters of the main model are used to estimate the downstream financial numbers for the holdout sample, given the favorability of perceptions observed among customers of this holdout sample. The estimated financial numbers are then juxtaposed with the actual observed financial numbers for the hold-out sample, and proximity between these two sets of numbers is used to provide support for the model's validity.

In one linkage assignment, the sponsoring firm was able to provide us with voluminous data on their large pool of customers, which allowed us the luxury of isolating a random holdout sample for validation. We ran the model on 70% of the total data and then used such modeling results to predict the financial numbers for the 30% holdout sample. The proximity between the predicted and the observed financial numbers for customers of the holdout sample significantly bolstered the confidence of the sponsoring firm in the results of the linkage analysis. In another vali-dation exercise, we used longitudinal data to demonstrate that the firm was able to retain more of its satisfied customers over time, and that these customers actually increased their spending with the firm over a year's time. The dissatisfied customers, on the other hand, were shown to be more likely to defect to other suppliers or reduce their level of spending with the firm.

Filter 9: Tailoring the Communication Strategy

Linking customer perceptions to their behavior often involves complex analyses, which creates a significant challenge in communicating the results to the users of such information. Business managers are less inter-ested in the analytics than they are in seeing a compelling and easy-to-understand link between customer attitudes and customer behavior. It is thus easy to lose their attention with analytically complex information, and it becomes important to present the analytical findings in a simple and meaningful way. The ability to present the required information in the format desired by these audiences is critical for soliciting their buy-in.

In one option that we frequently exercise, we typically classify each individual customer into categories of loyalty—low, medium, and high—based on the customer's score to a set of loyalty measures, such as "overall satisfaction." Then, for each of these categories, we show differences in mean revenue (or other financial measures of interest, such as share of wallet) that the customers provide to the firm to demonstrate the positive link between customer affinity and their business activity with the firm (Figure 9.5). This method of communication validates the positive link between customer perceptions and behavior observed in the analytical model, and makes it easier for business managers to estimate the financial gains associated with moving their customers from the less favorable to the more favorable levels of loyalty. Such a simplified communication strategy also makes it easier to get buy-in from these users of information for the overall linkage analysis program.

Filter 10: The Need to Cater to Two Sets of Audiences Throughout Results Dissemination

Typically, the customer-financial linkage analyses cater to two very different sets of audiences. One of these comprises senior level managers who

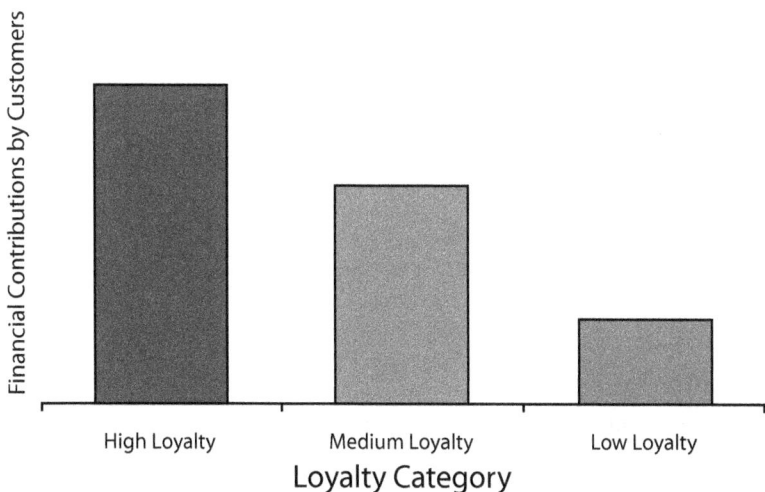

Figure 9.5. Customizing the communication strategy.

want empirical validation for a positive link between customer perceptions and behavior, to justify resource investments in CLRM programs. The other set comprises the frontline employees and managers who want more granular and specific information—for example, what should be done differently when the first customer walks in the next morning. Further, it is important for both these sets of audiences to work on the proposed improvement priorities in harmony with all other organizational initiatives so that the organization is working in tandem toward the common goal of improved customer loyalty in the marketplace.

In one research project, we catered to both these sets of audiences by linking transactional data (e.g., customer evaluations of support transactions) to the relational customer database (overall attitudes toward the firm), and then further linking the relational database to customer purchase data. The positive relationship between relational customer perceptions and customer behavior demonstrated that customers with more favorable perceptions also provide greater revenue to the firm. This catered to the needs of senior management and provided them with the required confidence to continue to invest in customer focused measurement programs. The link from the transactional to the relational database, and further to actual customer behavior, in turn helped identify the specific activities during each individual customer transaction that have the most significant impact on overall customer affinity levels, and therefore on the revenue and profits that the customers provide to the firm. For example, the analyses confirmed that specific actions, such as the ability of the firm to decrease "hold time," where a customer is put on hold while the agent confirms something, can have a much greater positive impact on customer experience vis-à-vis a similar reduction in "wait time"—the time a customer has to wait before an agent answers the call. This helped frontline employees to focus their priorities on areas that were most beneficial to the overall marketplace and to the financial health of the firm.

Concluding Thoughts

The overall intent of this chapter was to share a best-practice approach to linking various streams of data so that such linkages can be used for enhanced decision support. At the very least, we hope the reader can walk away from our discussion with an appreciation that such analyses require both—careful "art" blended with meticulous "science." The linkage process has low awareness and appreciation in the marketplace. In our experience, most such projects do not fail because they selected the wrong analytical tool for their purpose. Instead, an inability to follow a systematic yet customizable process often leads to such failure. For example, a lack of support from senior management is one of the most common and earliest warning signs that we witness. When such support is missing, inordinate amounts of effort are spent to assemble the appropriate stakeholders, and to get them to participate in the research project. Similarly, we strongly recommend that data limitations, if any, should be understood earlier in the process to allow for realistic expectations setting.

CHAPTER 10

Developing a Linkage Orientation

Mission, Vision, Linkage!

Overall, we propose that the formulation of marketing strategy within an organization should include a statement of its overall mission, a clear understanding of its vision of the future and a commitment to discovering the linkages between the vision and the portfolio of strategic choices. The articulation of the mission and vision statements set the higher order of direction, values, and goals for the organization. Thereafter the linkage discovery process helps convert these abstract objectives into a set of coherent actions that collectively constitute the execution of the organization's strategy. Linkages also generate the appropriate set of markers that can constitute a measurement and tracking system that can be used to continuously evaluate progress and assess what corrective actions are warranted. Interestingly, we find that while many medium and large organizations have formal processes to articulate their mission and vision statements, virtually none of them has even an informal process to discover the linkages between their strategic actions and short- or long-term goals. This discrepancy results in a wide gap between the mission and vision on the one hand and the set of strategic choices on the other.

We suggest that organizations can remove this deficiency by developing what we call a linkage orientation. Firms that embrace linkage orientation will be better able to understand the flow of relationships between their strategic choices and their downstream consequences. They will be in a stronger position to break down departmental silos and connect causes and effects across multiple organizational domains. Linkage-oriented firms will also be able to avoid metrics myopia and sharpen their focus on two extremities of flowprints: the strategic choice or action and the ultimate downstream financial consequence of interest. Finally, these firms will be able to bind their people more closely together because of a shared realization that the consequences of actions in one part of the organization have a web of effects on the others.

Developing a Linkage Orientation: A Ten-Step Approach

So what does it mean to have or develop a linkage orientation within an organization? As we have discussed throughout the book, data-driven discovery processes should govern strategic marketing choices and they should be relatively free from mental models and managerial intuition. We now provide a road map for firms to assess whether or not they are linkage oriented and for them to achieve such orientation.

Step 1: Challenge existing mental models. The starting point of developing a linkage orientation is the realization that entrenched mental models drive decision making within the organization or in any of its silos. A simple method of performing this check would be the process of asking your organizational mental models the 10 questions listed earlier. We believe that the resulting diagnosis might raise important questions about the use of a model beyond its half-life and about the presence or absence of reverse gears on the model or might simply validate the model for continued usage.

Step 2: Become paradigm free. The objective of developing linkage orientation is not to merely challenge existing mental models and discover alternatives but to encourage decision makers to think independently of them. Paradigms have their own limitations in terms of which firm they apply to, to what extent, and for how long. It is unlikely to be the case that one organization will discover a perfect strategic paradigm that will drive it over the course of its life or even for reasonably long periods. For example, we have witnessed several paradigms including innovation, relationship marketing, and outsourcing, and many others outlive their useful life inside organizations. Therefore, a key facet of a linkage-oriented organization is developing only loose ties to paradigms, and ultimately be willing to transition to a paradigm-free and data-driven world.

Step 3: Avoid metrics myopia. Most paradigms come with their own set of popular metrics. For example, customer centricity comes with measures of satisfaction and loyalty, while customer relationship management comes with estimates of share of wallet. Productivity-driven paradigms come with a variety of metrics, such as profits per square foot of store or shelf space or sales per employee. While these metrics have merit within the paradigm they emerge from, developing a linkage orientation involves a reduction in the emphasis on one or a set of metrics. Instead, what is important is an emphasis on flowprinting and a willingness to accept that the elements of a strategic flowprint may change, sometimes very significantly, over time and across strategic contexts. In other words, while linkage-oriented organizations are likely to deploy a set of metrics as part of the flowprinting process, they are not wedded to any of them and are willing to transition to new sets, as the data dictate and as the flowprints command.

Step 4: Shift strategic emphasis to flowprinting. A shift from metrics myopia to linkage orientation involves embracing the flowprinting process as a driver of strategic and market planning. Of course, this is easier said than done. Most organizations have embedded beliefs about causal relationships among variables that drive their business. Consequently, the shift toward a flowprint-driven planning process is psychologically difficult. However, it comes with several important advantages: First, it lets data rather than beliefs drive strategic decision making, and second, it makes the organization nimble and enables it to change and adapt as the flowprints evolve over time. For example, if increases in satisfaction are no longer the drivers of growth, a linkage-oriented organization is in a better position to make this discovery and rethink its strategic focus than an organization that is wedded to the satisfaction metric.

Step 5: Invest in the action-profit-linkage discovery process. We have discovered that one of the reasons that holds organizations back from data-driven strategy is the resource requirement. Most senior managers and C-level executives are not able to or willing to invest time, money, and human capital in the linkage discovery process. The notion of experimentation and hypothesis testing is foreign to them. The discovery of the linkages among actions and consequences is both involved and time consuming. It also requires substantial psychological resources because it often reveals relationships that are contrary to organizational beliefs and conventional wisdom. It also requires top management to have communication expertise because the rationale for changes in strategic direction, whenever warranted, needs to permeate the entire organization in order for everyone to align behind it. This is especially true when the relationships revealed by linkage analyses suggest changes in compensation structure and have a direct effect on people's own earning potential.

Step 6: Connect left to right. As we have noted, one of the fundamental premises of the action-profit-linkage approach is that organizations should strive to build and assess the relationships between the actions on the extreme left and the ultimate consequences on the extreme right. However, we find that most organizations are stuck in the middle. They focus on connections among intermediate metrics and constructs rather than on actions and consequences. An example would be a focus on the relationship between satisfaction and loyalty. In this case, the former is not an action and the latter is not an ultimate financial objective. Both are possibly intermediate points in a strategic flowprint that would start from an action that might influence satisfaction and end at a financial consequence. Therefore, in order to become linkage oriented, it is important for organizations to flowprint the connections between the extremities. Otherwise, they may end up devoting resources to strengthen intermediate relationships that may or may not be as important in connecting actions to financial consequences.

Step 7: Break organizational silos. One of the hallmarks of a linkage-oriented organization is the ability to break organizational silos and develop strategic flowprints that span multiple departments. As mentioned earlier, flowprinting allows decision makers to recognize that their function is part of an overall organizational network, and that cross-functional coordination is necessary to move the organization forward in a concerted fashion. Specifically, managers are more likely to adopt a cross-functional perspective when they can visually observe the linkages at an organizational level and where their departments and functions fit within the larger picture.

Step 8: Focus on decision equity. Ultimately, all strategic actions should be compared based on the financial consequences that are discovered through the flowprinting process. Therefore, while we do not advocate a focus on multiple, intermediate metrics, developing a linkage orientation does require a focus on the ultimate metric. We propose decision equity to be that metric. Comparing alternate investment options on this common metric provides decision makers with a fair and level comparison system for choosing actions that are conducive to the financial health of the organization. While some of these estimates might not be as accurate as these executives might desire, the ability to provide a comparison, with finite organizational resources, is a better option than making investment decisions using noncomparable metrics.

Step 9: Compete on linkages. We have not delved much on this issue in the book, but linkages and flowprints provide a foundation for strategic differentiation in the marketplace. The notion of strategic differentiation is analogous to, but somewhat different from, the more familiar notions of product or brand differentiation. All three share one common principle, and that is an emphasis on doing what others do not. For example, firms that aim for product differentiation attempt to configure their product offerings differently from how their competition does. They emphasize a different, and potentially a unique, set of product attributes that others either do not offer or find difficult to replicate. Similarly, when firms aim for brand differentiation, they attempt to endow their brands with unique brand values that become the basis of points of differentiation relative to competing brands. Once again, the emphasis is on separation of perceptual or abstract attributes in the minds of the customer.

We formulated the proposed concept of strategic linkage-based separation along the same lines. The objective of such separation is to have unique strategic flowprints, rather than unique product configurations or brand values. For example, consider two firms in the same industry, say fast food, competing in a similar customer space. Imagine that we build strategic flowprints for a similar set of actions for both firms. Let us say we pick investing $10 million in research and development for product improvement at each firm. Now the strategic flowprints corresponding to this common action for the two firms could turn out to be vastly different from one another or very similar. We would say that the firms have strategic separation if these flowprints are different either in terms of the structure or in the strength of the relationships among its various elements. In other words, flowprint separation would suggest that the consequences of common actions are different for the two firms. We propose that the hallmark of strategic separation is where the drivers of success vary across firms and ultimately lead to them executing very different portfolio of actions. The principles of benchmarking provide the opposing perspective. When firms benchmark, they are essentially comparing their performance with their peer group on the same metrics. We expect that a benchmarking-oriented mind-set would therefore lead to strategic convergence rather than strategic separation.

Now why is this important, and what does this have to do with linkage-orientation? First, let us begin by noting that while we have come across examples of many firms adopting and practicing product and brand differentiation, we have come across virtually none that explicitly practices or formulates strategy based on linkage separation. To that extent, most do not harness the power of linkage orientation. Now let us go back to what this means in terms of practice. First, as we note previously, linkage-based separation is contrary to the principles of benchmarking. When firms benchmark, they attempt to get similar levels of scores on similar sets of metrics that others employ. While this might perhaps be useful from the perspective of independent analysts or academics who are interested in comparing firms, it has its limitations from the perspective of the firms themselves. It forces them to pursue the same levels of performance on the same set of measures as the best in class or the industry standard. Consequently, perhaps unknowingly, it puts firms on a path of strategic similarity or parity rather than strategic separation and differentiation. Just like it makes little sense to build a parity brand, it should make little sense to build a parity strategy. In our view, benchmarking promotes strategic parity, while linkage orientation promotes strategic separation.

Further, competing on linkages means charting out distinct and unique strategic flowprints rather than imitating those of competitors. Conceptually, this is what is done for products and brands. The objective is to discover strategic fulcrums that are not the same as everyone's so that the drivers of success and the financial returns on success are differentiated. For example, if all personal financial advisory firms execute similar actions to acquire high net worth individuals, they are not strategically separated if the downstream consequences of these actions look similar for each one of them. Along the same lines, if the downstream consequences of choosing to focus on creditworthy individuals look similar for multiple credit card issuers, they are not strategically separated. The same principle can be extended for fast food chains and actions such as promoting value menus, or cellular providers for actions such as choosing bucket cellular plans. On the other hand, firms that are linkage oriented would attempt to ensure that their linkage flowprints are separated and that their portfolio of appropriate strategic actions is different from those of their competitors.

Step 10: Learn through linkages. Finally, one can view organizational learning from the perspective of decision equity and linkage analyses. While learning is a broad-based term, we wish to highlight two critical aspects within this context. First, one aspect of learning is gaining knowledge about the consequences of specific strategic actions. A learning organization would invest in developing a repository of linkage flowprints that would help guide future decisions and assist in enhancing decision equity over time. We find that while many organizations invest in products, processes, research and development (R&D), and marketing research, virtually none invests in strategic R&D and learning the functionality of strategic levers. It is difficult for the top management to come to terms with allocating resources that can optimize the short-term and the long-term downstream consequences of strategic decisions. However, we believe that those that do will build strategically nimble organizations that will be able to make superior and quick strategic choices.

Second, as organizations evolve and as the broader market conditions and business climate changes, so do the flowprints for success for individual firms. For example, the strategic flowprints for menu redesign for a restaurant are different when the economy is in an upswing versus when it is turning down. Similarly, the flowprints for success for credit card issuers are different when the financial markets are in a strong shape versus when they are not. The second aspect of learning is understanding the sensitivity of flowprints emanating from the same action but under different external circumstances. For example, the relative importance of customer satisfaction, customer retention, and brand portfolio consolidation are sensitive to external factors. It is therefore important for firms not only to build an overall repository of strategic flowprints but also to build them separately for different exogenous conditions in order to do a strategic sensitivity analysis around the decisions in question.

One Final Note

Developing a linkage separation requires a dramatic shift in the organizational thinking and decision-making processes. It calls for a reduced commitment to unverified existing models and paradigms, and their associated metrics. It promotes an emphasis on comparing alternate investment decisions on common downstream metrics. It requires building strategic flowprints that are adaptable to changing internal and external circumstances. And it needs psychological tenacity to be able to ask tough questions and demonstrate a willingness to exit strategy prisons created by well-entrenched mental models. However, it comes with numerous benefits. Linkage-oriented organizations are likely to be nimble and agile and demonstrate an increasing appetite for data-driven and fact-based decisions. They are more likely to take actions with positive decision equity, break functional silos or at least coordinate better across them, and provide their managers with better tools to address current and future marketing challenges.

Epilogue

The consultant looked at the confused faces all around him, especially the concerned look on the chief executive officer's face, and slowly began his address:

"I know that all of you are wondering what really happened here. Should the value of the firm have gone up by more than $20 million because of all the equity created here? Or is it that the net value created is just $20 million and there is actually less credit to go around than is being claimed? You would perhaps also wonder about where the credit really belongs if the second scenario is indeed true. In reality, where did we really create the equity? All of these are fair questions, and I will try to answer them as best as I can.

"Let me begin with the bad news. The total equity created is actually only $20 million. Because all of us were connected with this value creation, each one of us unknowingly claimed *all* of it. That led to double counting, triple counting, and so on and gave the impression that value was created independently in each domain and should be added up. But, realistically speaking, we collectively created that value and should not each claim full credit for it.

"Naturally, the next question is to whom the credit belongs. In order to answer this question, we should ask ourselves whether *we* made the decision that led to value creation or if we were beneficiaries of someone else's decision. From my vantage point, there are two critical decisions here. The first is the marketing vice president's decision to change the packaging of the flagship brand. The change in the brand's fortune is directly linked to this decision. To that extent, the packaging decision holds equity to the tune of $20 million. The fact that customers are now more valuable is a consequence of this decision and not an independent event. Similarly, the fact that the brand is more valuable today is also a consequence of the same decision. In other words, both customer equity and brand equity were beneficiaries of the decision to change packaging.

The true residence of equity is in the packaging decision. Therefore, the credit for value creation should go to the new vice president of marketing.

"However, there is one caveat, and this brings me to the second critical decision. I would be sympathetic to a claim from the vice president of human resources that the decision to change the packaging design was a consequence of her decision to alter the hiring policy and recruit from outside the industry. In other words, the equity really resides in her hiring decision, not in the packaging decision made by the newly hired vice president of marketing. There is some truth to that. However, another way to look at this issue is to state that the new hiring policy possibly increased the likelihood of good decisions. However, the vice president of human resources did not make the specific decision that led to value creation. In other words, her decision neither directly changed the stream of future cash flows for the company by enhancing revenues or reducing costs, nor reduced the size of the assets deployed by the company. To that extent, the equity resides primarily in the packaging decision. However, because the change in the hiring policy increased the odds of a good, value-enhancing decision, such as the actual packaging decision, perhaps some credit can be transferred to human resources. Over time, if we see a consistent linkage between the change in hiring policy and value creation, we will acknowledge hiring as a strategic fulcrum and transfer decision equity accordingly. In any event, the equity resides in one or perhaps two decisions, and the remaining entities are merely its beneficiaries.

"Finally, from a learning perspective, we discovered that product packaging is one of the key strategic fulcrums of our business. More importantly, we learned how to connect decisions to their *ultimate* outcomes and did not get mired in trying to improve the value of an intermediate metric. We also learned the cross-functional underpinnings of the effects of good decisions. To that extent, whether accidentally or deliberately, we took a first step toward becoming more integrated on the one hand and paradigm free on the other. That is not to say that we are now heading toward chaos just because we are beginning to abandon our long-standing mental models. On the contrary, we just discovered perhaps our first strategic fulcrum from perhaps our first strategic flowprint. If we continue down this path of verification-based management, we will ultimately build our own repository of actions that work and discover strategic fulcrums that matter in our business. This new knowledge base will be data driven, verification based, and unique to our company. We can slowly begin to leverage this accumulated knowledge to speed up our decision making, learn to discard weak options, and quickly converge on strong actions that are likely to work. In other words, we will ultimately build value for this firm by successively taking actions that have high decision equity."

The "Analytical Tools" of Linkage Analysis

Introduction

Now that we have perhaps made a case for firms to engage in linkage analysis and focus on decision equity, we would like to spend some time here discussing some of the simple but popular analytical tools that are used to link data. The scope of this discussion is not meant to be either exhaustive or technical because there are numerous textbooks that cover these topics in detail. Instead, our objective is to provide a nontechnical discussion of some basic techniques that the reader and potential user of linkage analysis can grasp in order to follow the logic underlying strategic flowprints and the interpretation of results. Our emphasis therefore is on providing enough information so that these users can be more familiar with alternate analytical options, and can become more sophisticated users and buyers of such research. More statistically inclined readers can skip this section very easily. For the rest of us, who could use a little more brushing up of our statistics fundamentals, read on! A good place to start will be to refresh some fundamentals of statistics that are foundational for understanding these analytical techniques.

An Important Distinction: Averages and Variation

Before ending into a discussion of the tools themselves, it is important to emphasize the distinction between two key characteristics of data. The first is average or the mean value of a specific variable. For example, managers are often interested in customer satisfaction scores. Let us assume that a firm collects data on satisfaction and some other attitudinal variables, each on a 7-point scale from 1000 of its customers. We find that most senior level managers and C-level executives are interested in the average values or means of the metrics they follow. In this case, for instance, managers are most likely to be interested in the average satisfaction score from the sample of 1000 customers. An average close to 6 or 7 will be treated favorably, while an average close to 3 or 4 will not. Some managers may also institute programs to track changes in these average satisfaction scores over time and design interventions when the numbers fall below a certain threshold. The focus on averages is perhaps understandable because the concept is easy to understand, compute, compare, and act upon. Even business cases largely present data in terms of mean values and that accentuates the focus on the measure.

However, statistical analysis is not only about means but also about variation. Much like the mean captures the midpoint of a data series, the variation captures its spread. For example, consider two cases where the average satisfaction scores were 5 on a 7-point scale. However, in one case they tended to vary between 4 and 6 and in the other case, they varied between 3 and 7. We would say that the second case had greater variation than the first even though both had the same average. Most analytical tools are designed to explain variation in one variable, or compare the variation between two or more variables. For example, if we need to understand the relationship between customers' waiting time in a queue and their overall satisfaction, we will need data on the variation of the two metrics. The appropriate statistical tool can then be used to examine whether there is any relationship between the variation in waiting time and the variation in satisfaction. Merely knowing the average waiting time and the average satisfaction score will be of little value. Once they understand the relationship between the variations of the two metrics, managers will be able to ask the appropriate "what if" questions. For instance, they will be able to assess the impact of reducing waiting time by 1 minute on satisfaction levels of the customers.

The need to deploy information on variation becomes even greater when we consider more than two variables. Continuing with the same example, let us say that managers at a firm have a hunch that their customer satisfaction depends on the waiting time and the attitude of the server. However, they do not know which one of the two, if any, is the stronger driver of satisfaction. Once again, the appropriate statistical tool will assess how much of the variation in satisfaction can be explained by variation in waiting times versus the variation in server attitudes. The result from the analysis will help managers link satisfaction with the two metrics and learn about the strength of the linkages. They could, in turn, use this information to make resource allocation decisions between initiatives to reduce waiting time versus those for improving server attitude. Once again, merely knowing the mean values of the three metrics will be of little use to either understand the drivers of satisfaction or make data-driven resource allocation decisions.

In the previous example, we have implicitly discussed a third data property relevant for our discussion. This property is "covariance" which is at the heart of techniques such as correlation, regression, and structural equations modeling that are broadly classified as covariance-based techniques. The key difference between "covariance" versus "mean" and "variance" is that while mean and variance can be computed for a single measure, covariance needs at least two measures to be computed. For example, we can compute the mean and the variance for the single measure of interest to us—the IQ of individual students. However, if we were interested in exploring the differences, if any, in the IQ of students by their income (or gender or any such demographic variable), then we would work with covariance. In this case, for example, we will examine how a particular measure, IQ in our case, varies with another measure, which could be the gender of the student. Therefore, anytime we are interested in the relationship between two measures, we examine how they covary with each other.

Most techniques used for linking different streams of data therefore come from the "covariance-based" family of analytical tools. "Correlation," "regression," and "structural equations modeling" are some of the tools you might have used or heard about in your projects, even if they were not related to linkage analysis. While we do not suggest that these three techniques are all that we will ever need to conduct linkage analysis, we focus on them for three reasons. One, we encounter these techniques most frequently in our engagements. Second, they collectively capture the essence of questions that managers typically need answered during linkage analysis. And third, in case the need arises, more sophisticated and powerful versions of each technique are available to address questions that are more complicated or to handle complex data. The purpose of this section is therefore to introduce these classes of techniques in a nonstatistical manner in order to increase the level of comfort and confidence in deploying them and dealing with their outputs.

Working With Covariation

When we talk of covariation, there are three essential things to consider: the direction, the strength, and the statistical significance of such covariation. Let us start with direction, and use another example for illustration. Suppose a market research agency is working on a project for a chain of stores that has not been very profitable in the recent past. Management has therefore undertaken certain initiatives to improve their profitability, and one of these pertains to productivity enhancements in the stores through workforce reduction. The research charter then is to ascertain the link between productivity and profitability. One school of thought could be that stores that are more productive will be more profitable in the long run because of the elimination of redundancies and reduction of the number of in-store employees. The other school of thought could be that fewer in-store employees will lead to less favorable customer experiences, which in turn will lead to customer exodus and therefore lower store profitability in the long run. From a statistical perspective, while both these arguments acknowledge that there is likely to be covariation between the measures of productivity and profitability, there is less certainty regarding the direction of the covariation: It could be positive or negative. Positive covariation means that as productivity goes up, profitability will go up too, while negative covariation means that as productivity goes up, profitability will go down.

After ascertaining the direction of the relationship, the next charter is to determine the strength of the relationship. In the previous example, then, if the analysis confirmed a negative relationship between productivity and profitability, the next analytical step is to determine its magnitude. Such magnitude estimation will help assess whether every percentage point increase in productivity would lead to a percentage point decrease in profit, or would it be smaller than or larger than a percentage point? Simply knowing that the relationship between productivity and profitability is negative is not going to provide much help to management. Instead, they would want to know the magnitude of this negative relationship is meaningfully large. While some of the covariance-based techniques such as regression analysis can help determine the magnitude, sometime simpler techniques such as correlation analysis can often provide an upper and lower bound for relationship strength.

Finally, when the direction and magnitude of covarying measures has been determined, we examine the statistical significance of the relationship. The purpose of this step is to assess whether the observed covariance relationship is true and authentic, or merely an outcome of chance. So if the observed relationship is being tested at a significance level at say 99%, in simple English it means that we are willing to accept a 1 out of 100 chance that the observed relationship does not exist in the real world (i.e., it is zero) and that we observe it simply out of chance. Thus if the analysis points to a significant relationship between variables, the analytical team can be 99% confident that the relationship is meaningfully different from zero, with only a 1% chance that the conclusion might erroneous. Most statisticians and analysts commonly use the confidence levels of 90%, 95%, or 99%, which means that they are willing to accept 10 in 100, 5 in 100, or 1 in 100 chances respectively of concluding that a meaningful relationship exists, when in reality it does not. However, an important point of caution when working with statistical significance is that the volume of data influences such conclusions. In the interest of keeping the discussion nontechnical, we will simply state that more volume of data gives greater power to data, and therefore increases the likelihood of finding statistically significant relationships. For a data set, say with a million records for example, a correlation coefficient of 0.05 (correlation coefficient can range from zero to one—a point we explain shortly) is very likely to be statistically significant. On the other hand, for a data set with 50 observations, even a correlation of 0.30 may not be significantly different from zero. Thus, as one reviews the statistical significance information, one has to be careful about the statistical versus the substantive difference. One needs to ask if 0.05 is substantively different from zero just because the difference is statistically significant. Conversely, one should make a similar argument and ask whether a correlation coefficient of 0.3 should be dismissed merely because it was not statistically different from zero.

The Three Essential Analytical Tools

Having discussed the basic data properties of mean, variance, and covariance, we not turn to discussing the three covariance-based techniques referenced earlier—correlation analysis, regression analysis, and structural equations modeling (SEM). We will discuss these in the same order, that is, correlation followed by regression and then followed by SEM. The reason for doing so is that correlation is probably the simplest to deploy and understand, and SEM is the most complex. However, simple does not mean inadequate or inferior to a more complex technique. Sometimes based on the objectives of the research, correlation might provide all the necessary information that the project requires. In such a case, it sometimes makes little sense to invest time and capital deploying a more complex technique such as SEM. Overall, our key objective in explaining these techniques is to provide readers with enough information on each so that they can be more astute buyers of research. They would be in a better position to ask hard questions regarding which of these techniques will be most applicable for their specific purpose.

Correlation Analysis

Correlation analysis is a covariance-based technique that is bivariate in nature. What this means is that when running correlation analysis, the focus is on only two variables at a time. Let us say a survey that asks hotel guests to provide their ratings of overall satisfaction with the stay, as well as their evaluations of various areas of experience such as room cleanliness, technology, room service, and fitness facilities. Correlation analysis can now be used to identify which of these experience areas have a greater impact on guest satisfaction. In such analyses, one would start by correlating guest ratings of overall satisfaction with performance ratings provided by guests about room cleanliness. The results would provide information on the three key parameters—the direction, magnitude and statistical significance of the correlation between the two variables. One could then run a similar correlation analysis between guest ratings of overall satisfaction and say their ratings of technology. The same analysis could then be repeated for other pairs of variables. At the end of such pair-wise analysis, each of these correlation outputs could be looked at simultaneously, to assess which of the areas of experience has a greater impact on overall guest satisfaction.

As would be obvious by now however, these analyses are bivariate because each correlation analyzes only two variables at a time—overall guest satisfaction and one individual area of experience. In running the correlation between overall guest satisfaction and say, room cleanliness, the analysis assumes that there is nothing else in the world that matters or changes. In other words, it assumes that other variables, such as room service, fitness facilities, and so on have no effect on the relationship between the two variables under study.

The correlation coefficient, the outcome of correlation analysis, is a number that can range between minus one and plus one. A minus or plus indicates the first of the three considerations—the direction of the relationship. A positive value of the correlation coefficient suggests that the two measures covary in the same direction—that is, if guests report favorable perceptions of room cleanliness, they are also likely to report favorable overall satisfaction with the stay. A negative correlation coefficient value on the other hand suggests that the measures move in the opposite direction—that is, more favorable perceptions of room cleanliness result in less favorable overall guest satisfaction. From the perspective of magnitude, the second consideration, a correlation coefficient is constrained between minus and plus one. A magnitude of one indicates that

Estimating the Relationship Between Two Variables	
Guest satisfaction (1–10) scale	Annual revenue ($) provided by guest
1	100
2	200
3	300
4	400
5	500
6	600
7	700
8	800
9	900
10	1000

there is a perfect association between two measures. In the previous table, for example, overall guest satisfaction would be estimated to have a plus one correlation with guest revenue, wherein every point improvement in overall guest satisfaction will lead to an incremental hundred dollars of revenue. On the other hand, a correlation coefficient of minus one will exhibit a similar perfect relationship but the variables will move in opposite directions. Less-than-perfect relationships lower the magnitude of the correlation coefficient. An absence of any relationship at all results in a correlation of zero.

Regression Analysis

Regression analysis is very similar to correlation, but has two key differences. One, regression allows a researcher to work with more than two measures at the same time, and can therefore expand the scope of analysis from a bivariate world to a multivariate world. If we continue with the hotel example discussed previously, regression analysis will not require the each potential driver of overall hotel guest satisfaction to be analyzed one at a time. Instead, it can allow the research team to simultaneously identify the relative importance of multiple areas of experience, such as room cleanliness, technology, room service, and fitness facilities, in one single and common model. From a consumer behavior perspective then, regression allows the research team to analyze a situation where the respondent can be seen as evaluating all these areas of experience simultaneously in providing an overall guest satisfaction rating. Such an underlying assumption, some could argue, is more consistent with the way things work in the real world. The following table shows how the concept of correlation analysis can be expanded to include multiple drivers of revenue provided by each guest.

The estimated parameter would confirm that every point improvement in guest satisfaction still leads to an incremental $100 of revenue. However, what the analysis would also provide as new information is that for a given level of satisfaction with the hotel stay, the total annual revenue provided is also contingent on the number of total annual business trips taken by the guest. In this case, every incremental business trip taken by the guest gives the hotel chain an opportunity to make an extra $50 from the guest.

Guest satisfaction (1–10) scale	Number of business trips taken annually	Annual revenue ($) provided by guest
1	5	350
2	5	450
3	5	550
4	5	650
5	10	1000
6	10	1100
7	10	1200
8	10	1300
9	20	1900
10	20	2000

This leads to the second of the two key differences between regression and correlation. Unlike correlation analysis, the estimated parameter value of regression analysis is not constrained say between minus one and plus one. Consequently, the research team can estimate the real financial impact of improving guest satisfaction, as well as that of targeting more frequent business travelers. This allows management to hypothesize and evaluate alternate scenarios. They can evaluate the impact of shifting focus to frequent travelers as well as the potential benefit of improving their current guest satisfaction rating by one scale point and so on.

Structural Equations Modeling

Structural equations modeling (SEM) is a relatively more recent analytical introduction to the tool kit of marketers. It is similar to regression analysis, in that it is a multivariate technique, and therefore has the ability to examine covariation among more than two measures as part of one overall model. There are however three important differences between regression analysis and SEM. One, SEM allows an analyst to work with latent constructs. An easy way to explain a "latent construct" is that it is a concept or phenomena that we cannot directly observe and are therefore unable to directly measure. Customer satisfaction is a good example of a latent construct. Theoretically speaking, satisfaction measures a customers' overall evaluation of their consumption experiences. However, one cannot directly observe something like "customer satisfaction." Therefore, we design a set of proxy measures to tap the concept. This often requires multiple measures that all tap into the common concept that we like to label as "customer satisfaction." In a survey, for example, we might ask customers to provide their responses on, say, a 1 to 10 scale on multiple measures of satisfaction such as "overall satisfaction," "expectations being exceeded," and "proximity to the ideal brand."

The second important difference between SEM and regression analysis is that the former acknowledges and incorporate measurement error into the models. In the interest of keeping the discussion nontechnical, we will skip the details, encouraging the interested readers to pick suitable texts on the topic. We would however make the point that such error is widespread in social sciences, and can often dilute the estimated relationships. Accounting for measurement error, as is provisioned for in SEM, allows the research team to boost the strength of the relationship among the variables of interest. Last but certainly not the least, SEM allows the research team to draw a structure of relationships among various measures, which is something regression analysis cannot perform. Imagine that the team believes that, in the market of interest, favorable pricing perceptions lead to more positive value perceptions, which in turn lead to greater customer satisfaction. SEM allows us to design and estimate such a series of relationships through one model. Regression analysis on the other hand will estimate the impact of price perceptions and value on customer satisfaction, without recognizing the price perceptions may themselves be driving value.

Selecting an Appropriate Technique

Now that we have described the fundamental characteristics of three commonly used analytical techniques that come from the covariance-based family of analyses, the natural next question is which of these is the best? Unfortunately, there is no easy answer, as the choice of the technique depends on both—the analytical objectives as well as the properties of the data available to estimate the relationships. As a very simple illustration, if the research objective is to assess the impact of overall guest satisfaction on the revenue provided by the guest, correlation analysis is unlikely to work. It is very plausible that if guest satisfaction is measured on a 1 to 10 scale, every point improvement is likely to have a revenue impact that is beyond the plus or minus one range presented by correlation analyses. Therefore, in this case, correlation analysis will not be able to answer the research objective. Instead, regression or SEM might be more appropriate.

Overall, while many considerations affect the choice of an appropriate analytical technique, we list some that are important in selecting an optimal tool. One key consideration is the need to perform simulations. As previously discussed, when simulations about likely scenarios are required correlation analyses do not suffice because they have a range restriction on the estimated strength of association. The second key consideration is whether consumer behavior in the industry is consistent with a bivariate technique or a multivariate technique. In other words, would most customers be evaluating various areas of experience one at a time, or would they be thinking of many things all at once. If the customer evaluation of the consumption experience is likely to be multivariate, then regression analysis and SEM will be preferred candidates.

A third key consideration is the volume of available data and the amount of missing data. Since correlation analysis is a bivariate technique that works through pairs of measures, it typically requires fewer data points, than multivariate techniques such as regression and SEM. Of the three analytical techniques discussed, SEM requires the largest sample size. From our experience, SEM models require about 15 to 20 times the number of data points as the number of measures in the model. Therefore, if a model has 20 measures in it, SEM might require 300 to 400 data points for estimation. While considering the available volume of data, it is also very important to estimate the *effective* base size. Missing data introduces the difference between available data and effective base size, especially for multivariate techniques. In typical multivariate techniques, if any measure that is included in the model has missing data, then the analysis excludes the observation from the computation—unless some form of missing data can be imputed. For example, if a model includes various drivers of satisfaction with a grocery-store visit, and one of the drivers included in the model is a measure with very low incidence, such as the availability of enough wheel chairs, then the model is likely to have lots of missing data for this measure. If the missing values cannot be imputed the effective base size available for analyses will be smaller. Last, but an equally important consideration, is the need to work with latent constructs, and the need to incorporate measurement error. When such a need exists, SEM might be the analytical tool of choice.

Recommendations

While we discussed a best-practice approach and process to linkage analysis in chapter 7, the intent of this section was to discuss the "science" of linkage analysis in nontechnical terms. We believe that both the science and art are very important for achieving successful outcomes from linkage analyses. However, because numerous textbooks describe the statistical tools we discuss here in detail, we kept our discussion at a nontechnical level to allow those of us who are less comfortable with analytical techniques to get a general grasp of the subject. The goal is to facilitate the marriage between the "art" and "science" of linkage analysis that would, in turn, encourage managers to take advantage of the data at their disposal to improve the quality of their decisions by connecting their actions to the ultimate terminal outcomes of interest.

Notes

Chapter 1

1. Fornell et al. (1996).
2. Spencer (2006).
3. Gantz et al. (2007).
4. IDC (2007)
5. Google search conducted on June 24, 2010.

Chapter 2

1. Nutt (1999).
2. Winerman (2005).

Chapter 3

1. Anthony et al. (2008).
2. Coyle and Matsumiya (2007).

Chapter 4

1. Hawn (2004).

Chapter 5

1. http://www.callcentermagazine.com/showArticle.jhtml?articleID=201000
2. Hansen and Singh (2008).

Chapter 6

1. Ittner and Larcker (2003).

Chapter 7

1. Kaplan and Norton (1992).
2. Heskett, Sasser, and Schlesinger (1997).
3. http://www.baldrige.nist.gov
4. Epstein, Kumar, and Westbrook (2000).
5. For the purpose of our discussion, we are defining "validity" as the property of the data to measure what it is truly intended to measure, and "reliability" as the ability of the measurement instrument to produce the same score over repeated measurement periods.

Chapter 8

1. Some of the numbers have been disguised, but the overall spirit of the case study has been preserved.

References

Anthony, S. D., et al. (2008). *Innovator's guide to growth: Putting disruptive innovation to work*. HBS Publishing.

Coyle R. E., & Matsumiya, T. (2007, Fall). Too much of a good thing: Quality as an impediment to innovation. *California Management Review, 50*(1), 77–93.

Epstein, M. K., Kumar, P., & Westbrook, R. A. (2000). The drivers of customer and corporate profitability: Modeling, measuring, and managing the causal relationships. *Advance in Management Accounting, 9*, 43–72.

Fornell, C., Johnson, M. D., Anderson, E. W., Jaesung Cha, & Bryant, B. E. (1996, October). The American customer satisfaction index. *Journal of Marketing, 60*, 7–18.

Gantz, J. F., et al. (2007, March). The expanding digital universe: A forecast of worldwide information growth through 2010. Retrieved from http://www .emc.com/collateral/analyst-reports/expanding-digital-idc-white-paper.pdf

Hansen, K., & Singh, V. (2008, October 10). Are store-brand buyers loyal? An empirical investigation. *Management Science, 54*, 1828–1834.

Hawn, C. (2004, January). If he's so smart . . . Steve Jobs, Apple, and the limits of innovation. *Fast Company, 78*(68).

Heskett, J. L., Sasser, W. E., & Schlesinger, L. A. (1997). *The service profit chain: How leading companies link profit and growth to loyalty, satisfaction, and value.* New York: The Free Press.

IDC. (2007, March). The expanding digital universe: A forecast of worldwide information growth technology. Retrieved from http://www.emc.com/ collateral/analyst-reports/expanding-digital-idc-white-paper.pdf

Ittner, C., & Larcker, D. (2003, November). Coming up short on nonfinancial performance measurement. *Harvard Business Review* (November, 2003), 88–85.

Kaplan, R. S., & Norton, D. P. (1992, January–February). The balanced score card—measures that drive performance. *Harvard Business Review* (January–February, 1992), 71–79.

Nutt, P. C. (1999). Surprising but true: Half of the decisions in organizations fail. *Academy of Management Executive, 13*(4), 75–90.

Spencer, S. (2006, February). *Leading CEOs: A statistical snapshot of S&P 500 leaders.* Retrieved from content.spencerstuart.com/sswebsite/pdf/lib/ 2005_CEO_Study_JS.pdf

Winerman, L. (2005). What we know without knowing how. *Monitor on Psychology, 36*(3), 50–52.

Index

Announcing the Business Expert Press Digital Library

Concise E-books Business Students Need for Classroom and Research

This book can also be purchased in an e-book collection by your library as

- a one-time purchase,
- that is owned forever,
- allows for simultaneous readers,
- has no restrictions on printing, and
- can be downloaded as PDFs from within the library community.

Our digital library collections are a great solution to beat the rising cost of textbooks. E-books can be loaded into their course management systems or onto student's e-book readers.

The **Business Expert Press** digital libraries are very affordable, with no obligation to buy in future years.

For more information, please visit **www.businessexpert.com/libraries**. To set up a trial in the United States, please contact **Sheri Allen** at *sheri.allen@globalepress.com*; for all other regions, contact **Nicole Lee** at *nicole.lee@igroupnet.com*.

OTHER TITLES IN OUR MARKETING STRATEGY COLLECTION
Series Editor: **Naresh Malhotra**

Developing Winning Brand Strategies by Lars Finskud

Conscious Branding by David Funk and Anne Marie Levis

Marketing Strategy in Play: Questioning to Create Difference by Mark E. Hill

www.ingramcontent.com/pod-product-compliance
Lightning Source LLC
Chambersburg PA
CBHW060541210326
41519CB00014B/3296